Vegetarian Visitor

Vegetarian Visitor 2010

Edited by Annemarie Weitzel

Jon Carpenter

to Shetlands

This edition first published 2010 by
Jon Carpenter Publishing, Alder House, Market Street, Charlbury, Oxfordshire OX7 3PH
Tel: 01608 819117 E-mail: vv@joncarpenter.co.uk
This compilation © Annemarie Weitzel
Whilst the publishers must disclaim responsibility for any inaccuracy, the information in
this guide has been carefully checked at the time of going to press
ISBN 978-1-906067-06-9
Printed and bound by Antony Rowe Ltd, Chippenham

Contents

How to use this guide

Welcome to the new edition of *Vegetarian Visitor*, listing private houses, guest houses, hotels, cafés, restaurants and pubs which take catering for vegetarians and vegans seriously. All establishments in the guide have been supplied with a 'We're in Vegetarian Visitor 2010' sticker, to make them easily recognisable.

Activity holidays, Special breaks, Courses

Entries are listed alphabetically by county, then name. Almost all offer bed and breakfast: 'see also page XX' tells you where to find further details, including websites and email addresses.

Accommodation and Eateries

Entries are grouped geographically in sections and within each section alphabetically by county, then town or village, then name. London is divided into Central, East, North, South and West and entries are arranged first by postcode (i.e. NW3, W1, WC2, SW16), then alphabetically by name.

Accommodation addresses have coded information as well as a general description. The codes indicate the following:

H Hotel	**G** Guest House	**PH** Private house

INS   Inspected under one of the schemes operating in Britain; full details can be obtained from the establishment concerned if required

L   Licensed

DA   Disabled access

V   Exclusively vegetarian: entries without this code also cater for non-vegetarians

Ve   Also catering for vegans; please mention you are a vegan when you contact the establishment

Vegan   Exclusively vegan

NS   No smoking anywhere on the premises (may include garden)

pNS   Smoking restricted to certain areas only

CN   Car necessary: a car/taxi journey or extended walk is needed from the nearest public transport

Acc2   Accommodation for two adults; children travelling with their parents can sometimes be accommodated additionally

Price categories for bed and breakfast per person per night (minimum, guide only):
CatA over £37.50; **CatB** £25-£37.50; **CatC** under £25.

Many cafés, restaurants and pubs have a short description, as well as coded information. Opening times may vary not only by establishment but also by season. As a general rule, cafés will be open during the day but not in the evening, and are often closed on Sundays and Bank Holidays. Restaurants are generally open for lunch and in the evening; they may be closed one day a week, but this is not usually Sunday. Pubs are normally open seven days a week and may be open all day and in the evening. If you want to be sure that your chosen eating place is open, please give them a ring. The codes give the following information:

R	Restaurant	**C**	Café	**P**	Pub
L	Licensed				

a   A selection of vegetarian dishes daily, as well as non-vegetarian food; quite often at least one vegan dish is also on the menu

b   Vegetarian food only

c   Vegetarian and vegan food only

d   Vegan food only

w   Wholefood

org   Organic produce used when possible

F   Fairtrade products used

As England, Wales and Scotland have a ban on smoking in public places, which includes restaurants, cafés and pubs, all premises are smoke-free.

I would be delighted to hear from any user of this guide. If you have stayed or eaten somewhere not listed, please drop me a line with the name and address and I will contact them for next year's edition.

Annemarie Weitzel
2 Home Farm Cottages, Sandy Lane, St Paul's Cray, Kent BR5 3HZ
email: a.weitzel@live.co.uk

Activity Holidays, Special Breaks, Courses

England

Nab Cottage
☎ 015394 35311, fax 015394 35493

Rydal, Ambleside, Cumbria LA22 9SD

Retreat breaks, workshops and courses in yoga, dance, massage, transforming cellular memory. The workshop/venue space in the attached barn is ideal for groups, yoga, dance, walking, celebrations. See also page 68.

Rothay Manor
☎ 015394 33605, fax 015394 33607

Rothay Bridge, Ambleside, Cumbria LA22 0EH

We offer the following types of specialised holidays: antiques, bridge, gardening, music, walking, painting, chess, scrabble, interior design, literary Lakeland. See also page 65.

Devon Valley Retreat
☎ 01548 821180

Lower Norris House, North Huish, South Brent, nr Totnes, Devon TQ10 9NJ

Feeling stressed?? Unwind in beautiful, hidden Devon valley. Aromatherapy massage, reflexology and spiritual healing available. Healing, painting and other courses held occasionally. Groups welcome. See also page 33.

Tor Cottage
☎ 01822 860248, fax 01822 860126

Chillaton, Devon PL16 0JE

We are a Romantic Retreat and a special place for Birthdays, Anniversaries and Honeymoons. Special Autumn-Spring Breaks available, offering one night free of charge, or 10% discount on a 7-night holiday throughout the year. No children. No smoking. No pets. See also page 31.

Cheltenham Lawn
☎ and fax 01242 526638

5 Pittville Lawn, Cheltenham, Gloucestershire GL52 2BE

We run art, design, textile and mixed media printmaking courses. See also page 53.

Claridge House, Quaker Centre for Healing, Rest and Renewal
☎ 01342 832150

Dormans Road, Dormansland, Lingfield, Surrey RH7 6QH

Open all year for stress releasing peaceful stays, rest, retreat and renewal. Courses with a spiritual, healing or creative focus. See also page 22.

Tekels Park Guest House
☎ 01276 23159, fax 01276 27014

Tekels Park, Camberley, Surrey GU15 2LF

We offer courses in theosophy, yoga, healing and various alternative therapies. See also page 22.

Wales

Pen Pynfarch
☎ 01559 384948

Llandysul, Carmarthenshire SA44 4RU

Courses in Body, Movement and Environment are available. See also page 87.

Over the Rainbow
☎ 01239 811155

Plas Tyllwyd, Tan-y-Groes, near Cardigan, Ceredigion SA43 2JD

We offer courses in salsa dancing, bellydancing, Reiki and yoga. See also page 88.

Awen Vegetarian B&B
☎ 01495 244615

Penrhiwgwair Cottage, Twyn Road, Abercarn, Newport, Gwent NP11 5AS

Please ask about our courses in Reiki I, II and III. See also page 86.

The Nurtons
☎ 01291 689253

Tintern, near Chepstow, Monmouthshire NP16 7NX

Courses by individual tutors on topics of their choice are offered, also retreats, healing etc. See also page 86.

Cuffern Manor
☎ 01437 710071

Roch, Haverfordwest, Pembrokeshire SA62 6HB

Contact us regarding Alexander technique, stitchcraft and Nordic waltzing courses. See also page 88.

Elan Valley Hotel
☎ 01597 810448, fax 01597 810824

Elan Valley, Rhayader, Powys LD6 5HN

We organise wild mushroom foraging, bird watching, watercolour landscapes and life drawing special breaks with expert tutors. See also page 83.

Primrose Earth Centre
☎ 01497 847636

Primrose Farm, Felindre, Brecon, Powys LD3 0ST

Quiet retreats are offered for de-stressing. Sound healing (UK College of Sound Healing) and food and health courses are also available. See also page 84.

Scotland

Creag Meagaidh B&B
☎ 01540 673798

Main Street, Newtonmore, Inverness-shire PH20 1DP

If you are interested in a running, walking, wildlife, skiing, cycling or multi activity holiday please contact us. See also page 100.

Fournet Guest House ☎ 01340 821428
Balvenie Street, Dufftown, Moray AB55 4AB

2009 was the year of conforming to rules and regulations and we can now move forward to offer wellbeing at its best for 2010. Please contact Alison for news of positive changes. She is hoping to teach and hand on her knowledge in Nutrition and Cooking particularly related to cancer. There are Norwegian Forest Therapy cats to stroke. There is a small library of fascinating and thought provoking books to dip into. Our new website will open up more possibilities and suggestions for your very special holiday. We look forward to seeing you in 2010. See also page 91.

London

Central London

Gloucester Place Hotel

☎ 020 7486 6166, fax 020 7486 7500

55 Gloucester Place, London W1U 8JQ

email: reservations@gloucesterplacehotel.com
website: www.gloucesterplacehotel.com

The Gloucester Place Hotel is a vegetarian-friendly Bed & Breakfast in Central London near Marble Arch, Oxford Street and many veggie restaurants. Most rooms are en-suite and offer satellite TV, hair dryer and tea & coffee tray. Check out our competitive tariff.
H CatB Ve pNS Acc50

Cafés, restaurants, pubs

Carnevale Restaurant ☎ 020 7250 3452
　135 Whitecross Street, London EC1Y 8JL　　　　　　R L c org F
Tas Restaurant ☎ 020 7430 9721/9722
　37 Farringdon Road, London EC1M 3JB　　　　　　R L a org
Zen Garden ☎ 020 7242 6128
　88 Leather Lane, London EC1N 7TT　　　　　　R/C L c F
Café Below ☎ 020 7329 0789
　St. Mary-le-Bow Church, Cheapside, London EC2V 6AU　　C L a F
Beatroot Café ☎ 020 7437 8591
　92 Berwick Street, Soho, London W1F 0QD
　Where else can you get proper veggie and vegan cooking like this? It's great value, with a big choice of delicious, healthy food.
　www.beatroot.org.uk　　　　　　C c w F
Hummus Brothers ☎ 020 7404 7079
　88 Wardour Street, London W1F 0TJ
　Hummus Bros serves freshly made hummus as a base with a selection of mouth-watering toppings accompanied by warm pitta bread. We offer mostly vegan and vegetarian dishes.　　　　　C a

GABY'S

30 Charing Cross Road
London WC2H 0DE
Tel : 020 7836 4233

La Porte des Indes ☎ 020 7224 0055
 32 Bryanston Street, London W1H 7EG   R L a
Mildreds ☎ 020 7494 1634
 45 Lexington Street, Soho, London W1F 9AN   R L c org
tibits Restaurant Bar Food to go ☎ 020 7758 4110
 12-14 Heddon Street, London W1B 4DA
 At tibits you create your own plate from more than 40 homemade hot
 and cold dishes from around the globe.   R/C L c w org
Gaby's Deli ☎ 020 7836 4233
 30 Charing Cross Road, London WC2H 0DE
 See display ad above.   R L a w
World Food Café ☎ 020 7379 0298
 1st Floor, 14 Neal's Yard, Covent Garden, London WC2H 9DP   C c

East London

Cafés, restaurants, pubs

Rootmaster ☎ 07912 389314
Ely's Yard, The Old Truman Brewery, Hanbury Street, London E1 6QL
R L d w org F

Wild Cherry ☎ 020 8980 6678
241-245 Globe Road, London E2 0JD
See display ad below. R c F

Pogo Café ☎ 020 8533 1214
76A Clarence Road, Hackney, London E5 8HB C d

North London

Cafés, restaurants, pubs

Jai Krishna Vegetarian Restaurant ☎ 020 7272 1680
161 Stroud Green Road, Finsbury Park, London N4 3PZ R c

Rasa N16 ☎ 020 7249 0344
    55 Stoke Newington Church Street, London N16 0AR   R L c
Café Seventy Nine ☎ 020 7586 8012
    79 Regents Park Road, London NW1 8UY   C b w org
Green Note ☎ 020 7485 9899
    106 Parkway, London NW1 7AN   R/C L c
inSpiral Lounge ☎ 020 7428 5875
    250 Camden High Street, London NW1 8QS
    Visionary vegan café serving soya and gluten free hot food, raw food, salads, raw cakes, truffles, vegan ice cream, smoothies, juices. Organic bar and music events.   C L d org F
Manna Restaurant ☎ 020 7722 8028
    4 Erskine Road, Primrose Hill, London NW3 3AJ   R L c org

South London

Bed and Breakfast Putney

☎ 020 8785 7609, fax 020 8789 5584

1 Fanthorpe Street, Putney, London SW15 1DZ

email: bbputney@btinternet.com
website: www.bbputney.com

Pip and Robert Taylor welcome you to a unique British experience. Our rooms are comfortable and reasonably priced. There is easy access to the centre of London. Putney has one of the best riverside locations, with attractive walks.
PH CatA Ve NS Acc4

Cafés, restaurants, pubs

Tas Pide ☎ 020 7928 3300
    20-22 New Globe Walk, London SE1 9DR   R L a
Tas Restaurant ☎ 020 7403 7200
    72 Borough High Street, London SE1 1XF   R L a
Mulberry Tea Rooms ☎ 020 8856 3951
    Charlton House, Charlton Road, Charlton, London SE7 8RE   C a org F
Domali Café ☎ 020 8768 0096
    38 Westow Street, Crystal Palace, London SE19 3AH   C L a
Shahee Bhelpoori ☎ 020 8679 6275
    1547 London Road, Norbury, London SW16 4AD   R L c

West London

The Temple Lodge Club

☎ 020 8748 8388, fax 020 8748 8322

51 Queen Caroline Street, Hammersmith, London W6 9QL

email: templelodgeclub@btconnect.com
website: www.templelodgeclub.com

The tranquility of this former home of Sir Frank Brangwyn is a peaceful haven providing respite after a busy day. The hearty breakfast is served overlooking our secluded garden, a view also enjoyed from the library and most bedrooms. Each has a washbasin, desk and tea-making facilities. Three rooms have showers; others share a shower-room and three bathrooms. Transport eastward takes you to The City and West End, westward to the Wetlands Centre, Kew Gardens and Richmond Park. VisitBritain 3 Stars.
G INS CatA V Ve NS Acc20

Cafés, restaurants, pubs

The Gate Vegetarian Restaurant ☎ 020 8748 6932
51 Queen Caroline Street, Hammersmith, London W6 9QL   R L c org F
222 Veggie Vegan Restaurant ☎ 020 7381 2322
222 North End Road, London W14 9NU   R L d w org F
Hollyhock Café ☎ 020 8948 6555
Terrace Gardens, Richmond Riverside, Richmond TW10 6UX
Beautiful little café with verandah overlooking the Thames in Victorian flower garden. Salads, pastries, soups, ices and chilled drinks served all day.   C c

Tide Tables ☎ 020 8948 8285
Riverside, Richmond TW9 1TH
Wonderful setting on banks of River Thames at Richmond. Delicious salads, bakes and snacks, smoothies, ice cream and gourmet coffees and teas served all day. www.tidetablescafe.com   R/C c org

Middlesex

Cafés, restaurants, pubs

Good Veg ☎ 020 8357 1740
62 High Street, Edgware HA8 7EJ   R c org
Pradip's Restaurant ☎ 020 8909 2232
156 Kenton Road, Harrow HA3 8AZ   R c
Pallavi South Indian Restaurant ☎ 020 8892 2345
Unit 3, Cross Deep Court, Heath Road, Twickenham TW1 4QJ
                                                   R L a

South and South East

Dorset (East)

Cowden House   ☎ 01300 341377
Frys Lane, Godmanstone, Dorchester DT2 7AG

website: www.cowdenhouse.co.uk

A spacious house on the edge of a little village, with beautiful views and surrounded by rolling downland. We provide a peaceful environment with comfort, personal attention and the highest quality vegetarian food, using local organic produce wherever possible. PH CatA V Ve NS CN Acc6

Cafés, restaurants, pubs

The Salad Centre ☎ 01202 393673
   667 Christchurch Road, Bournemouth BH7 6AA   R/C c w org F
Wessex Tales ☎ 01202 309869
   20 Ashley Road, Boscombe, Bournemouth BH1 4LH   R L d org F
Filippo's Italian Restaurant ☎ 01202 738031
   222 Ashley Road, Parkstone, Poole BH14 9BY   R L a

Hampshire

The Barn Vegan Guest House ☎ 023 8029 2531
112 Lyndhurst Road, Ashurst SO40 7AU

email: info@veggiebarn.net
website: www.veggiebarn.net

We offer exclusively vegan accommodation in a unique and beautiful area of the UK. We provide holidays with a light environmental footprint by, for example, generating nearly all of our electricity and using chemical-free household products.
G CatB Vegan NS Acc4

Cafés, restaurants, pubs

The White Horse ☎ 01489 892532
  Beeches Hill, Bishops Waltham SO32 1FD   P L a
Allsorts Psychic Café ☎ 023 8023 7561
  22 Carlton Place, Southampton SO15 2DY   C c
The Art House Gallery Café ☎ 023 8023 8582
  178 Above Bar, Southampton SO14 7DW   C L c w org F

Isle of Wight

Brambles ☎ 01983 862507
10 Clarence Road, Shanklin PO37 7BH

email: vegan.brambles@virgin.net
website: www.bramblesvegan.co.uk

See display ad on page 21.
G CatB Vegan NS Acc14

Cafés, restaurants, pubs

Quay Arts ☎ 01983 822490
  Sea Street, Newport PO30 5DB   C L a org F

Kent

Cafés, restaurants, pubs

Café Mauresque ☎ 01227 464300
8 Butchery Lane, Canterbury CT1 2JR   R L a
The Good Food Café ☎ 01227 456654
1-2 Jewry Lane, Canterbury CT1 2RP   C c org F
The India Restaurant ☎ 01303 259155
1 The Old High Street, Folkestone CT20 1RJ
Authentic traditional Indian home cooking. Freshly cooked, grease-
free and prepared to order.   R L a
What The DickInns Public House ☎ 01634 409912
1 Ross Street, Rochester ME1 2DF
See display ad on page 23.   P L a org
Brockhill Country Park Café ☎ 07798 752555
Sandling Road, Saltwood, nr Hythe CT21 4HL
Junction 11 off M20. Children's play area, a beautiful lake, walks and
savoury food at savery prices. We are open 10.30-5.30 April to October,
10.30-4 November to March, closed 22 December-4 January.   C c

Surrey

Tekels Park Guest House

☎ 01276 23159, fax 01276 27014

Tekels Park, Camberley GU15 2LF

email: ghouse.tekels@btclick.com
website: www.tekelspark.co.uk

Surrounded by 50 acres, we have
23 bedrooms and a hall for yoga
etc (available on an hourly, daily or
weekly basis). The Garden Room
Restaurant, serving delicious
vegetarian cuisine, is also open to
non residents. Booking is essential.
See also page 10.

G CatA DA V Ve NS Acc30

Claridge House

☎ 01342 832150

Dormans Road, Dormansland, Lingfield RH7 6QH

email: welcome@claridgehousequaker.org.uk
website: www.claridgehousequaker.org.uk

Victorian country house, beautiful gardens, open all year. Peaceful

stays, retreats, spiritual,
healing or creative courses.
Vegetarian house. Vegan and
certain medical diets
available with notice.
Disabled access. Ground
floor bedrooms available. No
single person surcharge. 46
minutes London Victoria.
See also page 10.

G CatA DA V Ve NS Acc17

WHAT THE DickInns

Feel confident the food served here really is vegetarian. Brenda, joint proprietor and strict vegetarian, prepares the food herself and also provides a limited menu for your carnivore friends! Wheelchair friendly and only 4 minutes from Rochester High Street with an attractive garden for eating al fresco with a glass of organic wine on those balmy evenings.

For further information contact Brenda or Graham on ~
01634 409912 ~ "What the DickInns Bar", Ross Street,
Off Delce Road, Rochester, Kent ME1 2DF

Cafés, restaurants, pubs

Riverside Vegetaria ☎ 020 8546 7992
  64 High Street, Kingston upon Thames KT1 1HN   R L c

For restaurants in Richmond, Surrey, please see under West London on pages 17/18.

Sussex

Dacres   ☎ 01323 870447
Alfriston, East Sussex BN26 5TP

Pretty country cottage in beautiful gardens in picturesque village. Sleeps two/three. Organic vegetarian breakfasts. En-suite bathroom. Colour TV. Tea/coffee making facilities. Near to South Downs Way, Glyndebourne, Seven Sisters, Charleston Farmhouse, village pubs, restaurants. Wonderful walking country. See us on www.alfriston-village.co.uk/accommodation
PH INS CatB Ve NS CN Acc3

Paskins Town House

☎ 01273 601203, fax 01273 621973
18/19 Charlotte Street, Brighton, East Sussex BN2 1AG

email: welcome@paskins.co.uk
website: www.paskins.co.uk

See display ad on page 25.
H INS CatA Ve NS Acc32

The Royal Hotel

☎ 01323 649222

8-9 Marine Parade, Eastbourne, East Sussex BN21 3DX

email: info@royaleastbourne.org.uk
website: www.royaleastbourne.org.uk

AA 4-star rated luxury B&B in prime seafront location overlooking the beach. One minute's walk to pier and town centre. Totally vegetarian with freshly squeezed juices, fruit salads and a selection of continental breads. Free high speed WiFi, dog friendly, eco-friendly (Green Tourism Member), gay friendly, smoke-free. Special rates for long stays. 5% discount for people who found us through this guide.
G INS CatA V Ve NS Acc20

Cafés, restaurants, pubs

Food for Friends ☎ 01273 202310
17-18 Prince Albert Street, The Lanes, Brighton, East Sussex BN1 1HF
                                                   R L c w org F

Infinity Foods Café ☎ 01273 670743
50 Gardner Street, Brighton, East Sussex BN1 1UN   C c w org F

Iydea ☎ 01273 667992
17 Kensington Gardens, Brighton, East Sussex BN1 4AL   C L c w org F

Terre à Terre ☎ 01273 729051
71 East Street, Brighton, East Sussex BN1 1HQ
Dining at Terre à Terre is a culinary experience like no other, with intense flavours and sublime textures few have the imagination or dare to put together. Website www.terreaterre.co.uk   R L c F

Café Paradiso ☎ 01243 532967
5 The Boardwalk, Northgate, Chichester, West Sussex PO19 1AR   C c

St Martin's Organic Tearooms ☎ 01243 786715
3 St Martin's Street, Chichester, West Sussex PO19 1NP   C L a org

Seasons of Lewes ☎ 01273 473968
199 High Street, Lewes, East Sussex BN7 2NS   R c org F

Wealden Wholefoods Co-op ☎ 01892 783065
High Street, Wadhurst, East Sussex TN5 6AA   C L c w org F

West Country

Cornwall

Coast
☎ 01736 795918

St Ives Road, Carbis Bay, St Ives TR26 2RT

email: info@coastcornwall.co.uk
website: www.coastcornwall.co.uk

Stylish B&B, exclusively vegetarian
and vegan, all rooms en-suite,
stunning sea views and garden.
Home to the hugely popular Bean
Inn Restaurant and Wild Planet
Art Gallery. Close to St Ives
beaches, restaurants and galleries.
G CatB V Ve NS Acc16

Westaways
☎ 01822 833745

Latchley, nr Gunnislake PL18 9AX

email: westaway.westaway@googlemail.com

Just 2½ miles from
Gunnislake and with
Tavistock, Plymouth and
Bude within easy reach,
Westaways is a lovely 17th
century cottage. We have
two double bedrooms for
guests and provide B&B
with lunches and evening
meals optional. Walks and
meditation on a quiet
peaceful retreat.

PH CatB V Ve pNS CN Acc4

Keigwin Farmhouse

☎ 01736 786425

near Morvah, Penzance TR19 7TS

email: gilly@yewtreegallery.com
website: www.yewtreegallery.com

Traditional farmhouse in West Cornwall on the St Ives to Land's End coast road. Glorious position overlooking the sea; sandy cove walking distance. Home-cooked, organic food. Guests' own parlour with open fire and piano. Extensive gardens and art gallery in the grounds. Photos via email.
PH CatB V Ve NS CN Acc5

The Great Escape

☎ 01736 794617

16 Parc Avenue, St Ives TR26 2DN

website: www.g-escape.freeuk.com

Chintz-free B&B fifteen minutes from the Tate Gallery. Stunning views of St Ives Harbour and Bay. En-suite rooms with TV and CD players. Full breakfasts including freshly squeezed orange juice, full veggie/vegan fry-up and home-made yoghurt and muesli.
G INS CatB V Ve NS Acc8

Making Waves

☎ 01736 793895

3 Richmond Place, St Ives TR26 1JN

email: simon@making-waves.co.uk
website: www.making-waves.co.uk

Making Waves have scaled back on the B&B accommodation they offer whilst bringing up their young family, but do now offer self-catering accommodation in two beautiful apartments with gardens, with the same stunning views and 2-minute walk to the

harbour. B&B off-season by arrangement. No more evening meals, but St Ives is spoilt for veggie-friendly cafés and restaurants Simon can point you towards!
Self-catering/G off-season INS CatB Vegan NS Acc6

Michael House   ☎ 01840 770592
Trelake Lane, Treknow, Tintagel PL34 0EW
email: info@michael-house.co.uk
website: www.michael-house.co.uk

Vegetarian and vegan guest house, near Tintagel, beach and coastpath nearby, lovely scenery and views, great sunsets. Evening meals, relaxing atmosphere, friendly and welcoming, open all year. Special Christmas breaks and spring and autumn offers. Children and pets welcome.
G CatB L V Ve NS CN Acc6

Boswednack Manor   ☎ 01736 794183
Zennor, St Ives TR26 3DD
email: boswednack@ravenfield.co.uk
website: www.boswednackmanor.co.uk

Peaceful farmhouse B&B, also self-catering cottage, near Zennor. Lovely views from all rooms. Library, organic gardens, friendly hens, sea sunsets. Wonderful walks, secret coves, wildflowers, stone circles. Pub ½ mile. Bus stops at gate. 100% vegetarian. Sorry, no dogs.
G INS CatC V Ve NS Acc10

Cafés, restaurants, pubs
The Bean Inn ☎ 01736 795918
   Coast B&B, St Ives Road, Carbis Bay, St Ives TR26 2RT
   See display advert on page 30.   R/C c org
Potager Garden ☎ 01326 341258
   High Cross, Constantine, Falmouth TR11 5RF   C c w org F
Café Cinnamon ☎ 01326 211457
   4-6 Old Brewery Yard, High Street, Falmouth TR11 2BY   C L c org F
Pea Sook Café ☎ 01326 317583
   19c Well Lane, Church Street, Falmouth TR11 3EG   R/C L c w org F

The Golden Lion Inn and Lakeside Restaurant ☎ 01209 860332
    Stithians Lake, Menherion, near Redruth TR16 6NW   R/P L a org F
Archie Browns Café ☎ 01736 362828
    Old Brewery Yard, Bread Street, Penzance TR18 2EQ   C L c org F
Waves Restaurant ☎ 01841 520096
    Higher Harlyn, St Merryn, Padstow PL28 8SG   R/C L a
The Crooked Inn ☎ 01752 848177
    Stoketon Cross, Trematon, nr Saltash PL12 4RZ   P L a org F
Fodders Restaurant ☎ 01872 271384
    Pannier Market, Back Quay, Truro TR1 2LL   R L a w org F

Devon

Cuddyford B & 'BEES'   ☎ 01364 653325
Rew Road, Broadpark, Ashburton TQ13 7EN

email: a.vevers@csl.gov.uk
website: www.ashburton.org/directory/cuddyford

Rural setting within Dartmoor National Park. Ideal for exploring Dartmoor, Dart Valley and South Devon coastline. Wholesome cookery – home-baked bread, free-range eggs, honey from our own hives, organic fruit and vegetables. Special diets catered for. Children are welcome.

PH INS CatB V Ve NS CN Acc4+small children

Tor Cottage   ☎ 01822 860248, fax 01822 860126
Chillaton PL16 0JE (Tavistock/Dartmoor area)

email: info@torcottage.co.uk
website: www.torcottage.co.uk

Nestling in private valley, relaxed romantic atmosphere. Luxurious beautiful bedsitting en-suites with own log fires and private gardens in streamside setting. Superb vegetarian breakfasts. Vegetarian owner. RAC 5 Diamonds Little Gem Award, National winner ETC Gold Excellence Award, 2002 All England Winner of AA Best Accommodation Award. Heated outdoor pool. Brochure available. Early booking advisable. See also page 9.

G INS CatA Ve NS CN Acc10

Lee House

☎ 01598 752364

27-28 Lee Road, Lynton EX35 6BP

email: info@leehouselynton.co.uk
website: www.leehouselynton.co.uk

See display ad above.
G INS CatB L Ve NS Acc16

Fern Tor Vegetarian and Vegan Guest House

☎ 01769 550339

Meshaw, South Molton EX36 4NA

email: veg@ferntor.co.uk
website: www.ferntor.co.uk

Surrounded by splendid countryside. Relax in our 12 acres or explore Exmoor, North and Mid-

Devon. En-suite. Cordon Vert host. Pets welcome. Voted Best Vegan Accommodation 2007, and one of *The Guardian*'s 10 Best UK Vegetarian B&Bs 2008.
G CatB V Ve NS Acc6

Sparrowhawk Backpackers ☎ 01647 440318
45 Ford Street, Moretonhampstead, Dartmoor National Park TQ13 8LN

email: ali@sparrowhawkbackpackers.co.uk
website: www.sparrowhawkbackpackers.co.uk

Beautifully converted stone stable, this is a small friendly, charming, eco-hostel located in the village of Moretonhampstead. A convenient base to explore the atmospheric Dartmoor National Park. Hiking, cycling, mountain biking, climbing, and wild swims here for the adventurous traveller. There is a fully equipped kitchen, solar heated showers, bike shed and lovely courtyard. Individuals, groups, families. Dorm or double room.
PH INS CatC DA Acc18

Devon Valley Retreat ☎ 01548 821180
Lower Norris House, North Huish, South Brent, near Totnes TQ10 9NJ

email: touchofheaven888@yahoo.co.uk
website: www.devon-valley.com

Unwind in tranquil, green valley 8 miles from Totnes. Enjoy the lovely views from the house or relax by the log fires. Wonderful walking area. Delicious vegetarian/vegan home cooking, special diets catered for. Healing, massage

and other therapies available on request. See also page 9.
PH INS CatB V Ve NS CN Acc6

Berkeley's of St James ☎ and fax 01752 221654
4 St James Place East, The Hoe, Plymouth PL1 3AS

email: enquiry@onthehoe.co.uk
website: www.onthehoe.co.uk

Quiet exclusive bed & breakfast offering free range/organic food where

possible. Ideally situated
on the Hoe, walking
distance to Sea Front,
Historic Barbican, Ferry
Port, Theatre, Pavilions
and City Centre and
within travelling
distance of the Eden
Project and Dartmoor
National Park.
G INS CatB NS CN
Acc10

The Old Forge ☎ 01803 862174
Seymour Place, Totnes TQ9 5AY

email: enq@oldforgetotnes.com
website: www.oldforgetotnes.com

A warm and friendly 600-year-old stone building with cobbled drive
and coach arch leading into a
walled south-facing garden.
Quiet and peaceful, yet close
to town centre and river.
Cottage-style rooms,
conservatory lounge with
whirlpool spa. Parking, free
internet access.
G INS CatA L Ve NS Acc20

Cafés, restaurants, pubs

The Terrace Café ☎ 01626 832223
  Devon Guild of Craftsmen, Riverside Mill, Bovey Tracey TQ13 9AF
  C L a w org F

The Courtyard Café & Wholefood Shop ☎ 01647 432571
  76 The Square, Chagford TQ13 8AE   C c w org F

Herbies Restaurant ☎ 01392 258473
  15 North Street, Exeter EX4 3QS   R L c F

The Plant Café-Deli ☎ 01392 428144
  1 Cathedral Yard, Exeter EX1 1HJ
  Contemporary vegetarian and organic food. Private dinner parties and
  outside catering available. Finalists in 2005 Vegetarian Society Awards
  'Best Café'.   C c w org F

The Country Table Café ☎ 01626 202120
  12 Bank Street, Newton Abbot TQ12 2JW   R/C a

Peter Tavy Inn ☎ 01822 810348
  Peter Tavy, nr Tavistock PL19 9NN
  See display ad below.   P L a

Willow Vegetarian Garden Restaurant ☎ 01803 862605
87 High Street, Totnes TQ9 5PB   R L c w org F

Dorset (West)

Cafés, restaurants, pubs
The Green Yard Café ☎ 01308 459466
4-6 Barrack Street, Bridport DT6 3LY   C L a w org F
Broadwindsor Craft and Design Centre ☎ 01308 868362
Broadwindsor, nr Beaminster DT8 3PX   R L a
Pilot Boat Inn ☎ 01297 443157
Bridge Street, Lyme Regis DT7 3QA   P L a

Somerset and Bristol

Marlborough House

☎ 01225 318175, fax 01225 466127

1 Marlborough Lane, Bath BA1 2NQ

email: mars@manque.dircon.co.uk
website: www.marlborough-house.net

See display ad on page 37.
G INS CatA L DA V Ve NS Acc16

Number 30

☎ and fax 01225 337393

30 Crescent Gardens, Bath BA1 2NB

email: david.greenwood12@btinternet.com
website: www.numberthirty.com

Three minutes' level walk to historical city centre and private parking.
Victorian, non-smoking house with a clean, contemporary feel.
Comfortable, light en-suite bedrooms. Superb English or great
vegetarian breakfasts. 'Outstanding housekeeping with a warm
welcome.' Weekends 2 night minimum.
G INS CatA Ve NS Acc8

Marlborough House

An enchanting, warm and friendly Victorian Town House, close to Royal Crescent, Assembly Rooms, Guild Hall, Roman Baths and Thermal Spas. All rooms are en-suite, spacious and unique, elegantly furnished with antiques, some with four-poster beds.
Breakfasts are generous, vegetarian and organic.

1 MARLBOROUGH LANE, BATH BA1 2NQ
TEL 01225 318175 FAX 01225 466127
mars@manque.dircon.uk   www.marlborough-house.net

Tordown B&B and Healing Centre

☎ 01458 832287, fax 01458 831100

5 Ashwell Lane, Glastonbury BA6 8BG

email: info@tordown.com
website: www.tordown.com

Victorian house situated on the southern slopes of Glastonbury Tor. Warm welcoming sacred space, in which you can relax and enjoy your stay. Beautiful rooms with tea, coffee, herbal tea, TV, en-suite. Healing and hydrotherapy spa available.
Sumptuous vegetarian/vegan breakfast provided. VB 4 Stars.
G INS CatB V Ve NS CN Acc12

Parsonage Farm

☎ 01278 733237

Over Stowey, Bridgwater TA5 1HA

email: suki@parsonfarm.co.uk
website: www.parsonfarm.co.uk

Traditional 17th-century farmhouse and organic smallholding in the Quantock Hills. Friendly and informal, with delicious meals using farm's produce, home-made breads and jams. Peaceful village, log fires and walled gardens make your stay a relaxing break, while being ideally situated for rambling and exploring the unspoiled Quantock Hills, Exmoor, North Somerset coast, Glastonbury and Wells.
G INS CatB Ve NS CN Acc6

Exmoor House

☎ 01643 841432

Wheddon Cross, Exmoor National Park, near Minehead TA24 7DU

email: info@exmoorhouse.com
website: www.exmoorhouse.com

Escape to Exmoor: award-winning, *Guardian*-recommended guest house in the heart of the National Park. Perfect for exploring, walking, cycling, relaxing. Tea and home-made cake on arrival, delicious dinners and breakfasts for vegetarians and non-vegetarians (gluten- and dairy-free food available too).
G INS CatA L NS Acc12

Cafés, restaurants, pubs

Demuths Vegetarian Restaurant ☎ 01225 446059
2 North Parade Passage, off Abbey Green, Bath BA1 1NX
Bath's only vegetarian restaurant, lots of vegan and gluten-free choices, organic wines. Open for breakfast, lunch, tea and dinner.
www.demuths.co.uk   R L c org F

The Porter ☎ 01225 404445
15 George Street, Bath BA1 2EN
See display ad below.   P L c
Sally Lunn's Refreshment House ☎ 01225 461634
4 North Parade Passage, Bath BA1 1NX   R L a
Tilleys Bistro ☎ 01225 484200
3 North Parade Passage, Bath BA1 1NX
Family-run city centre bistro close to Bath Abbey. French and English
cooking. Yummy vegetarian dishes. Gluten-free options available.
www.tilleysbistro.co.uk   R L a
Walrus & Carpenter ☎ 01225 314864
28 Barton Street, Bath BA1 1HH   R L a
Yum Yum Thai Restaurant & Café ☎ 01225 445253
17 Kingsmead Square, Bath BA1 2AE   R/C L a org F
Café Kino ☎ 0117 924 9200
3 Ninetree Hill, Bristol BS1 3SB   C L d org F

Café Maitreya ☎ 0117 951 0100
89 St Mark's Road, Easton, Bristol BS5 6HY
'Dazzling vegetarian food with attitude and edge in an unshowy
setting' - *Which? Good Food Guide*. Fine vegetarian and vegan cooking.
Website www.cafemaitreya.co.uk   R L c org

Friary Café ☎ 0117 973 3664
9 Cotham Hill, Cotham, Bristol BS6 6LD   C a

Rajpoot Restaurant ☎ 0117 973 3515
52 Upper Belgrave Road, Clifton, Bristol BS8 2XP   R L a

Royce Rolls Café ☎ 07967 211870
The Corn Exchange, St Nicholas Market, Bristol BS1 1JQ   C c w org F

The Thali Café ☎ 0117 942 6687
12 York Road, Montpelier, Bristol BS5 6QE
Serving delicious, organic, seasonal Asian dishes in the heart of
Bristol for over a decade. Vegans well catered for.   R L c org

Yum Yum Thai Restaurant & Café ☎ 0117 929 0987
50 Park Street, Bristol BS1 5JN   R/C L a org F

The Garden Café ☎ 01373 454178
16 Stony Street, Frome BA11 1BU   R/C L c w org F

Café Galatea ☎ 01458 834284
5A High Street, Glastonbury BA6 9DP
Established 16 years – internationally known
restaurant/gallery/cybercafé. High class vegetarian/vegan cuisine,
organic wines and beers. Open daytime and evenings. Website
www.cafegalatea.co.uk   R/C L c w org F

Rainbows End Café ☎ 01458 833896
17A High Street, Glastonbury BA6 9DP   C c w org F

Lotus Flower Thai Restaurant ☎ 01823 324411
89-91 Station Road, Taunton TA1 1PB   R L a org F

The Wheatsheaf ☎ 01454 412356
Chapel Street, Thornbury, near Bristol BS35 2BJ
Wide selection of home-made vegetarian and vegan dishes prepared
by the vegan co-owner of this traditional pub.   P L a

The Crown at Wells & Anton's Bistrot ☎ 01749 673457
Market Place, Wells BA5 2RP
Fifteenth-century inn providing affordable accommodation in the
heart of Wells. Fabulous food served every day, with great vegetarian
choices.   R/P L a

The Good Earth ☎ 01749 678600
4-6 Priory Road, Wells BA5 1SY   R L c w org F

Wiltshire

Cafés, restaurants, pubs

Circle Restaurant ☎ 01672 539514
High Street, Avebury SN8 1RF   R L c w
The Bistro & Cookery School ☎ 01380 720043
7 Little Brittox, Devizes SN10 1AR   R L a w org F
The Cross Keys Inn ☎ 01672 870678
16 High Street, Great Bedwyn, Marlborough SN8 3NU   P L a
Anokaa Contemporary Indian Cuisine ☎ 01722 414142
60 Fisherton Street, Salisbury SP2 7RB
Anokaa Restaurant recreates the classic fine dining experience in a
relaxing and welcoming way, embracing a passion for value and
excellence. www.anokaa.com   R L a org

Thames and Chilterns

Bedfordshire

Cafés, restaurants, pubs

Donatello's ☎ 01525 404666
91 Dunstable Street, Ampthill MK45 2NG — R L a org
Donatello's ☎ 01582 475797
204A High Street North, Dunstable LU6 1AU — R L a org
Dancing Lion ☎ 01582 666148/661485
1 Tring Road, Dunstable LU6 2PX — R L a

Berkshire

Cafés, restaurants, pubs

The Swan Inn ☎ 01488 668326
Lower Green, Inkpen, nr Hungerford RG17 9DX — R/P L a w org F
Tutu's Ethiopian Table at The Global Café ☎ 0118 958 3555
35-39 London Street, Reading RG1 4PS — R L a org F
Misugo Japanese Restaurant ☎ 01753 833899
83 St Leonards Road, Windsor SL4 3BZ — R L a w

Buckinghamshire

Cafés, restaurants, pubs

Carlos's Portuguese Restaurant ☎ 01296 423021
7-11 Temple Street, Aylesbury HP20 2RN — R L a
Malebon Lebanese Restaurant ☎ 01296 484010
21 Kingsbury Square, Aylesbury HP20 2JA — R/C a w org F

Hertfordshire

Cafés, restaurants, pubs

Woody's Restaurant ☎ 01442 266280
19 Dickinson Quay (Unit 1), Apsley Lock, Hemel Hempstead HP3 9WG
An authentic vegetarian restaurant, with all food cooked on the premises using predominantly organic and locally grown produce. Open every day through to the evenings. Vegan and gluten-free dishes available.   R/C L c w org F

Lussmanns Eatery ☎ 01727 851941
Waxhouse Gate, off High Street, St Albans AL3 4EW   R L a org F

The Waffle House ☎ 01727 853502
Kingsbury Watermill, St Michaels Street, St Albans AL3 4SJ
                                                     R/C a w org F

Oxfordshire

Cafés, restaurants, pubs

Tiffins Tandoori ☎ 01235 537786/550157
5-7 Bath Street, Abingdon OX14 3QH
See display ad on page 44.   R L a

The Magic Café ☎ 01865 794604
110 Magdalen Road, Kidlington OX4 1RG   R/C c

Tiffins Tandoori ☎ 01865 372245
63 High Street, Kidlington OX5 2DN
See display ad on page 44.   R L a

Café Moma ☎ 01865 813814
Modern Art Oxford, 30 Pembroke Street, Oxford OX1 1BP   C L a

Chiang Mai Kitchen ☎ 01865 202233
Kemp Hall Passage, 130A High Street, Oxford OX1 4DH   R L a

Edamame ☎ 01865 246916
15 Holywell Street, Oxford OX1 3SA   R L a

Hi-Lo Jamaican Eating House ☎ 01865 725984
68-70 Cowley Road, Oxford OX4 1JB
Open daily 7pm to 2am. Delicious organic vegan meals, snacks, Caribbean specialities. Tropical, Fairtrade, organic and local produce. Opened 1981.   R/C/P L a org F

The Nosebag Restaurant ☎ 01865 721033
6-8 St Michael's Street, Oxford OX1 2DU   R L a
Vaults & Garden ☎ 01865 279112
University Church of St Mary, High Street, Oxford OX1 4AH
                                                   C L a org F

Wyatts ☎ 01608 684990
Great Rollright, near Chipping Norton OX7 5SH   R/C L a

East Anglia

Cambridgeshire

Cafés, restaurants, pubs

The Cambridge Blue ☎ 01223 471680
  85/87 Gwydir Street, Cambridge CB1 2LG   P L a

Michaelhouse Café ☎ 01223 309147
  The Michaelhouse Centre, St Michael's Church, Trinity Street,
  Cambridge CB2 1SU   C L a

Rainbow Vegetarian Café ☎ 01223 321551
  9A Kings Parade, opposite Kings College gates, Cambridge CB2 1SJ
  World-famous, award-winning purely vegetarian and vegan restaurant,
  serving international innovative cuisine in the heart of historic
  Cambridge.   R/C L c

Essex

Cafés, restaurants, pubs

The Lemon Tree ☎ 01206 767337
  48 St Johns Street, Colchester CO2 7AD   R L a org

A Pinch of Veg ☎ 020 8590 0644
  751-753 High Road, Seven Kings IG3 8RN
  See display ad on page 46.   R L c

Norfolk

Number 15 Vegetarian Bed and Breakfast   ☎ 01603 250283

15 Grange Road, Norwich NR2 3NH

email: ianry2@hotmail.com
website: www.number15bedandbreakfast.co.uk

Number 15 is an environmentally-friendly place, where you can enjoy
vegetarian food prepared from local/organic/fairly traded produce. In

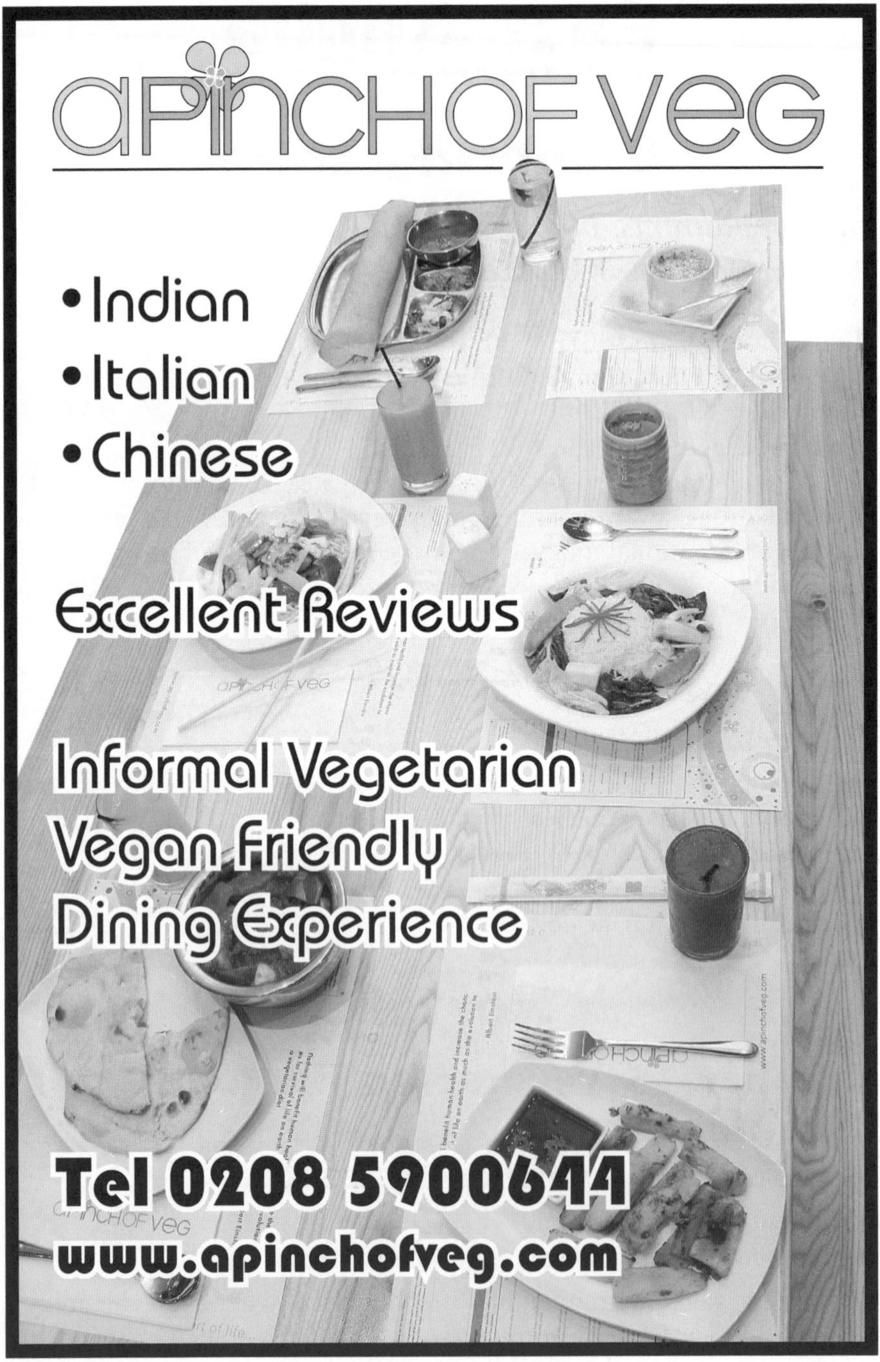
aPINCHOF VEG
• Indian
• Italian
• Chinese
Excellent Reviews
Informal Vegetarian
Vegan Friendly
Dining Experience
Tel 0208 5900641
www.apinchofveg.com

a quiet tree-lined street a short walk from the city centre and university. Ring Ian for more information.
G CatB V Ve NS Acc4

Greenbanks Hotel & Country Restaurant
☎ 01362 687742

Swaffham Road, Wendling, nr Dereham NR19 2NA

email: jenny@greenbankshotel.co.uk
website: www.greenbankshotel.co.uk

Country hotel with vegetarian menu plus meat cuisine, all using local produce. 10 acres of lakes and meadows, large indoor heated swimming pool, jaccuzi and sauna. Full disabled access with luxury wet rooms in ground floor suites. Pets welcome. Silver Awards, Green Globe Tourism Awards, Queens Awards for Environment.
H INS CatA L DA Ve NS Acc22

Cafés, restaurants, pubs

The Kings Arms ☎ 01263 740341
Westgate Street, Blakeney, Holt NR25 7NQ   P L a org

Amandines ☎ 01379 640449
Norfolk House Courtyard, St Nicholas Street, Diss IP22 4LB   R/C L c

The Greenhouse ☎ 01603 631007
42-46 Bethel Street, Norwich NR2 1NR
Norwich's environment centre. Open Tuesday-Saturday 10am-5pm, hot food from noon. Soups, savouries, cakes, Fairtrade, organic and local. www.GreenhouseTrust.co.uk   C L c w org F

Norwich Arts Centre ☎ 01603 660352
St Benedicts Street, Norwich NR2 4PG   C L a org F

Olive's ☎ 01603 230500
40 Elm Hill, Norwich NR3 1HG   C L a F

The Waffle House Restaurant ☎ 01603 612790
39 St Giles Street, Norwich NR2 1JN   R L a w org F

Suffolk

Western House ☎ 01787 280550
High Street, Cavendish CO10 8AR

In lovely village, this old coaching house is well placed for visiting villages of Lavenham, Kersey and Long Melford, and for gardeners there is Beth Chatto's by Colchester. Cavendish has three pubs which serve food in the evening.
PH CatC V Ve NS Acc7

Cafés, restaurants, pubs

Six Bells Inn and Restaurant ☎ 01359 250820
   The Green, Bardwell, Bury St Edmunds IP31 1AW   R/P L a
The Linden Tree ☎ 01284 754600
   7 Outnorthgate, Bury St Edmunds IP33 1JQ   R/P L a F
The Red Lion ☎ 01473 657799
   Greenstreet Green, Great Bricett, Ipswich IP7 7DD
   Family-friendly vegetarian pub, vegan and gluten-free choices. Large garden, play area, disabled access and facilities. Well-behaved dogs welcome.   P L c
Kwan Thai Restaurant ☎ 01473 253106
   14 St Nicholas Street, Ipswich IP1 1TJ   R L a

East Midlands

Derbyshire

Birds Nest Cottage Guest House

☎ 01457 853478

40 Primrose Lane, Glossop SK13 8EW

email: birdsnestcottage@btconnect.com
website: www.birdsnestcottage.co.uk

Accommodation with large woodland garden and riverside location. We provide a friendly welcome to modern facilities in a traditional environment. All rooms are en-suite or have private facilities. Your host is a qualified therapist offering massage, stones, Reiki, Hopi candles, reflexology.
G CatB Ve NS Acc9

Sheriff Lodge

☎ 01629 760760

Dimple Road, Matlock DE4 3JX

email: info@sherifflodge.co.uk
website: www.sherifflodge.co.uk

Luxurious accommodation in our guesthouse, with seven foot long beds. Our vegetarian breakfast offers a wide variety from which you can choose. We also cater for vegans and coeliac sufferers. We are only minutes from Chatsworth and the Peak District.
G INS CatA Ve NS Acc13

Cafés, restaurants, pubs

Columbine Restaurant ☎ 01298 78752
7 Hall Bank, Buxton SK17 6EW

R a

Scarthin Café ☎ 01629 823272
Scarthin Books, The Promenade, Scarthin, Cromford, near Matlock
DE4 3QF   C c w org F
The World Peace Café ☎ 01283 732338
Ashe Hall, Ash Lane, Etwall DE65 6HT
Set in 38 acres of tranquil grounds, the World Peace Café offers
Fairtrade coffee, speciality teas and a lunch menu.   C b F
Outside Café ☎ 01433 651936 ext. 3
Main Road, Hathersage, Hope Valley S32 1BB   C L a F
Thailand No 1 ☎ 01629 584444
43 Dale Road, Matlock DE4 3LT   R L a
Caudwell's Country Parlour ☎ 01629 733185
Rowsley, Matlock DE4 2EB   C c w org F

Leicestershire

Cafés, restaurants, pubs

The Good Earth Restaurant ☎ 0116 262 6260
19 Free Lane, Leicester LE1 1JX   R L c
Kayal ☎ 0116 255 4667
153 Granby Street, Leicester LE1 6FE
Authentic South Indian cuisine with lots of vegetarian choices. Old
Halli menu and more. www.kayalrestaurant.com   C L a w
Mirch Masala ☎ 0116 261 0888
Unit 19/20 Belgrave Commercial Centre, Belgrave Road, Leicester
LE4 5AU   R L c
Sakonis ☎ 0116 261 3113
2-16 Loughborough Road, Leicester LE4 5LD   R c
Staunton Stables Tea and Luncheon Rooms ☎ 01332 864617
The Ferrer's Centre, Staunton Harold, nr Ashby-de-la-Zouch LE65 1RU
The original Tea Room here at Staunton Harold. Tourism Award
winner, purveyors of fine food and beverages. Lunchtime reservations
recommended.   C a

Lincolnshire

Cafés, restaurants, pubs

The Five Sailed Windmill & Tea Room ☎ 01507 462136
East Street, Alford LN13 9EQ
One of the gems of rural Lincolnshire. Healthy eating in the stylish Tea Room. Beautiful working windmill producing stone-ground flours. Website www.fivesailed.co.uk and email enquiries@fivesailed.co.uk   C b w org F

Pimento Tearooms ☎ 01522 544880
26/27 Steep Hill, Lincoln LN2 1LU
Home-made vegetarian and vegan meals and cakes, plus a comprehensive list of leaf teas and freshly roasted and ground coffees.   C c

Thailand No 1 ☎ 01522 537000
80-81 Bailgate, Lincoln LN1 3AR
Authentic Thai cuisine, awarded 'Thai Select'. Exotic, healthy, delicious dining – Thai style. Private parties up to 40 people. Close to the cathedral and castle. Visit our website - www.thailandnumber1.co.uk   R L a

The Copper Kettle ☎ 01754 767298
29 Lumley Road, Skegness PE25 3LL   R L a F

The Five Sailed Windmill, Alford, Lincolnshire.

Cafés, restaurants, pubs

Alley Café/Bar ☎ 0115 955 1013
Cannon Court, Longrow, Nottingham NG1 6JE   C/P L c w org F
Annies Burger Shack at The Old Angel Pub ☎ 0115 947 6735
7 Stoney Street, Nottingham NG1 1JL
See display ad below.   P L a
Encounters Restaurant ☎ 0115 947 6841
59 Mansfield Road, Nottingham NG1 3FH   R L a
Squeek ☎ 0115 955 5560
23-25 Heathcote Street, Nottingham NG1 3AG
A relaxed and comfortable place to eat vegetarian and vegan food
freshly prepared from local organic produce.   R L c org F
Thailand No 1 ☎ 0115 958 2222
16 Carlton Street, Nottingham NG1 1NN   R L a
Minster Refectory ☎ 01636 815691
Minster Centre, Church Street, Southwell NG25 0HD
A selection of vegetarian dishes always available. Pre-booked parties
catered for. Outside catering also available.   C L a w F

Heart of England

Gloucestershire

Cheltenham Lawn Hotel and Pittville Gallery
☎ and fax 01242 526638

5 Pittville Lawn, Cheltenham GL52 2BE

email: anthea.millier@cheltenhamlawn.com
website: www.cheltenhamlawn.co.uk

Regency town house, close to Pittville Park, Pump Room, town centre, racecourse. Recently refurbished, original features, four-poster bed. Conference room, art gallery. Art/textile courses available. Member of the Vegetarian Society's Food and Drink Guild. Award-winning breakfasts. Wireless internet. See also page 10.
G INS CatB V Ve NS CN Acc10 (children on request)

Cafés, restaurants, pubs

Balti Spice ☎ 01453 766454
   17 Gloucester Street, Stroud GL5 1QG   R L a
Mills Café/Bar & Kitchen Shop ☎ 01453 752222
   Witheys Yard, High Street, Stroud GL5 1AS   C L a w org F

Herefordshire

Somerville House ☎ 01432 273991, fax 01432 268719
12 Bodenham Road, Hereford HR1 2TS

email: enquiries@somervillehouse.net
website: www.somervillehouse.net

See display ad below.
G INS CatA L DA Ve NS Acc20

Cafés, restaurants, pubs

The Pandy Inn ☎ 01981 550273
  Dorstone, nr Hay-on-Wye HR3 6AN   P L a org
Café @ All Saints ☎ 01432 370415
  All Saints Church, High Street, Hereford HR4 9AA   C L a w org
'Nutters' ☎ 01432 277447
  Capuchin Yard, Church Street, Hereford HR1 2LR
  See display ad on page 55.   C L c

Shropshire

White House Vegetarian Bed and Breakfast ☎ 01691 658524

Maesbury Marsh, Oswestry SY10 8JA

email: whitehouse@maesburymarsh.co.uk
website: www.maesburymarsh.co.uk

See display ad on page 56.
PH INS CatA DA V Ve NS Acc6+2 children

Cafés, restaurants, pubs

Cinnamon Coffee & Meeting Place ☎ 01746 762944
Waterloo House, Cartway, Bridgnorth WV16 4EG
All our food is freshly made. Catering for vegans, vegetarians, meat eaters, gluten-free, dairy-free etc. Great views! C L a F

Acorn Wholefood Café ☎ 01694 722495
26 Sandford Avenue, Church Stretton SY6 6BW
Award-winning highly commended long-standing wholefood café.
Central location in 'walkers welcome' town. Tranquil tea garden.
Open 9.30-5pm, closed Wednesdays.   C a w org F

Berry's ☎ 01694 724452
17 High Street, Church Stretton SY6 6BU   C L a org F

The Sun Inn ☎ 01584 861239
Corfton, Craven Arms SY7 9DF
Real ales suitable for vegans. At least one vegan and three vegetarian
meals on offer. Full disabled facilities.   P L a

The Olive Branch Restaurant & Coffee House ☎ 01584 874314
2/4 Old Street, Ludlow SY8 1NP   R/C L a org F

Raphaels Restaurant ☎ 01952 461136
4 Church Street, Shifnal TF11 9AA   R L a

The Goodlife Wholefood Restaurant ☎ 01743 350455
73 Barrack's Passage, Wyle Cop, Shrewsbury SY1 1XA
     R/C L c w org F

Monks Barn Farm ☎ 01789 293714

Shipston Road, Stratford-on-Avon CV37 8NA

email:
ritameadows@btconnect.com
website:
www.monksbarnfarm.co.uk

A delightful farmhouse offering
first-class amenities with views
across the Stour Valley. Ground
floor rooms available in the
Garden Annexe. Double/family/
twin/single rooms with en-suite
facilities. Riverside walks to the
village of Clifford Chambers.
G INS CatB Ve NS CN Acc6

Cafés, restaurants, pubs

Summersault ☎ 01788 543223
   27 High Street, Rugby CV21 3BW   R/C L c w org F
The Vintner ☎ 01789 297259
   4-5 Sheep Street, Stratford-upon-Avon CV37 6EF   R/Wine bar L a
Saffron Gold Restaurant ☎ 01926 402061
   Unit 1, Westgate House, Market Street, Warwick CV34 4DE   R L a

West Midlands

Cafés, restaurants, pubs

Al Frash Butterfly Balti Restaurant ☎ 0121 753 3120
186 Ladypool Road, Sparkbrook, Birmingham B12 8JS   R a org F
Jyoti Restaurant ☎ 0121 778 5501
1045 Stratford Road, Hall Green, Birmingham B28 8AS   R c
Kopper Khazana ☎ 0121 551 0908
12 Holyhead Road, Handsworth, Birmingham B21 0LT   R L a
The Warehouse Café ☎ 0121 633 0261
54-57 Allison Street, Digbeth, Birmingham B5 5TH
City centre oasis for vegetarians and vegans. Inexpensive good quality
food, plenty of choice in laid-back surroundings.   R/C c w org F
Browns Independent Bar ☎ 024 7622 1100
Earl Street, Coventry CV1 5RU
A family owned and run bar. One minute's walk from Coventry
Cathedral. www.brownsindependentbar.com   C L a

Kakooti Italian Restaurant ☎ 024 7622 1392
16 Spon Street, Coventry CV1 3BA   R L a org F

Garden Organic Restaurant & Café ☎ 024 7630 8213
Wolston Lane, Ryton on Dunsmore, Coventry CV8 3LG
See display ad on page 58.   R/C L a org

Worcestershire

Cafés, restaurants, pubs

The Green Dragon ☎ 01684 572350
126 Guarlford Road, Malvern WR14 3QT   R/P L a

Lady Foley's Tea Room ☎ 01684 893033
Great Malvern Station, Imperial Road, Malvern WR14 3AT   C L c F

Red Lion ☎ 01684 564787
4 St Anns Road, Great Malvern WR14 4RG   R/P L a org

Chesters Restaurant ☎ 01905 611638
51 New Street, Worcester WR1 2DL   R L a F

North East England

Cleveland

Cafés, restaurants, pubs

Eliano's Italian Brasserie ☎ 01642 868566
20-22 Fairbridge Street, off Grange Road, Middlesbrough TS1 5DJ
R L a

The Waiting Room ☎ 01642 780465
9 Station Road, Eaglescliffe, Stockton-on-Tees TS16 0BU   R L c w org F

Northumberland

Cafés, restaurants, pubs

The Tans Vegetarian Restaurant ☎ 01434 656281
11 St Mary's Chare, Hexham NE46 1NQ   R b
The Chantry Tea Rooms ☎ 01670 514414
9A Chantry Place, Morpeth NE61 1PJ   C L a

Tyne & Wear

Cafés, restaurants, pubs

Sky Apple Café ☎ 0191 209 2571
182 Heaton Road, Heaton, Newcastle upon Tyne NE6 5HP   R/C c F

Yorkshire

Beck Hall
☎ 01729 830332

Cove Road, Malham, near Skipton, North Yorkshire BD23 4DJ

email: alice@beckhallmalham.com
website: www.beckhallmalham.com

Eighteenth-century pet and child friendly Beck Hall welcomes visitors to the Yorkshire Dales. Situated by a stream and surrounded by countryside, there are 2 pubs nearby for dinner. Vegetarian home-cooked breakfasts and packed lunches.

H INS CatB L Ve NS Acc34

Marine View Guest House
☎ 01723 361864

34 Blenheim Terrace, Scarborough, North Yorkshire YO12 7HD

email: info@marineview.co.uk
website: www.marineview.co.uk

Ian and Virginia welcome you to their friendly, family-run six bedroomed guest house. Set in a prominent position on the North cliff overlooking the magnificent North Bay. All of Scarborough's numerous attractions are within easy walking distance.
G INS CatB Ve NS CN Acc15

Avondale Guest House ☎ 01904 633989
61 Bishopthorpe Road, York YO23 1NX
email: kaleda@avondaleguesthouse.co.uk
website: www.avondaleguesthouse.co.uk

Charming 19th-century
Victorian House just a few
minutes' walk to York's
ancient city walls. Homely
en-suite rooms with
extensive breakfast menu
including vegetarian
options. Non-smoking
environment with free on-
road parking. Prices from
£31 pp/pn. Minimum
booking two nights.
G INS CatA Ve NS Acc14

Cafés, restaurants, pubs

South Square Vegetarian Café ☎ 01274 677028
South Square, Thornton Road, Thornton, Bradford, West Yorkshire
BD13 3LD   C c org F
The Malt Shovel Inn ☎ 01423 862929
Main Street, Brearton, Harrogate, North Yorkshire HG3 3BX   R/P L a
'Bean There' ☎ 01262 679800
10 Wellington Road, Bridlington, East Yorkshire YO15 2BG
C b w org F

Brook's Restaurant ☎ 01484 715284
6 Bradford Road, Brighouse, West Yorkshire HD6 1RW   R L a
Eating Whole ☎ 01302 738730
25 Copley Road, Doncaster, South Yorkshire DN1 2PE
Small, friendly vegetarian and vegan café/restaurant with varied and
imaginative selection, all prepared and cooked on the premises.
R/C L c w org

Thai Elephant Restaurant ☎ 01423 530099
Unit 3-4, 13-15 Cheltenham Parade, Harrogate, North Yorkshire
HG1 1DD   R L a F

Relish ☎ 01422 843587
Old Oxford House, Albert Street, Hebden Bridge, West Yorkshire
HX7 8AH   R c org F
Hitchcock's Vegetarian Restaurant ☎ 01482 320233
1-2 Bishop Lane, Hull, East Yorkshire HU1 1PA   R L c F
Zoo Café ☎ 01482 494352
80B Newland Avenue, Hull, East Yorkshire HU5 3AB   C c F
Pollyanna's Tearoom ☎ 01423 869208
Jockey Lane, Knaresborough, North Yorkshire HG5 0HF   C a org
Hansa's Gujarati Vegetarian Restaurant ☎ 0113 244 4408
72/74 North Street, Leeds, West Yorkshire LS2 7PN   R L c org
Little Tokyo ☎ 0113 243 9090
24 Central Road, Leeds, West Yorkshire LS1 6DE
How can vegan food taste so good and with so many varieties under
one roof? They even do vegan wines & green tea latte… Come for the
experience…   R L a
Roots & Fruits ☎ 0113 242 8313
10/11 Grand Arcade, Leeds, West Yorkshire LS1 6PG   C b F
Lockwoods Restaurant ☎ 01765 607555
83 North Street, Ripon, North Yorkshire HG4 1DP   R/C L a
Nutmeg Vegetarian Café ☎ 01723 503867
93 Victoria Road, Scarborough, North Yorkshire YO11 1SP
Since 2006, Nutmeg Café has gained a local reputation for good,
wholesome home-cooked food. Daytimes only. Near the station.
                                                             C L c w org F
Airy Fairy ☎ 0114 249 2090
239 London Road, Sheffield, South Yorkshire S2 4NF
We offer a unique experience. Alongside our café and garden we have
a giftshop specialising in local and Fairtrade crafts.   C c w org F
Blue Moon Café ☎ 0114 276 3443
2 St James Street, Sheffield, South Yorkshire S1 2EW   C L c F
The Fat Cat ☎ 0114 249 4801
23 Alma Street, Sheffield, South Yorkshire S3 8SA
Award-winning city pub, 150-year-old listed building. Beer garden.
Vegetarian and vegan dishes a speciality. Menu changes weekly.   P L a
'Homemade' ☎ 07774 013438
4 Netheredge Road, Sheffield, South Yorkshire S7 1RU
Home-made vegetarian and vegan food, Monday 9.30-3.30, Tuesday-
Thursday 9.30-4pm, Friday 9.30-2.30 and 7pm-10.30, Saturday 9.30-

3pm and Sunday 9.30-2pm. Also bistro-style evening bookings for 10-22 people with a 2 or 3 course menu. C c

Nirmal Tandoori Restaurant ☎ 0114 272 4054
189-193 Glossop Road, Sheffield, South Yorkshire S10 2GW R L a

Le Caveau Restaurant ☎ 01756 794274
86 High Street, Skipton, North Yorkshire BD23 1JJ R L a

Wild Oats Café ☎ 01756 790619
10 High Street, Skipton, North Yorkshire BD23 1JZ C b w F

Dandelion and Burdock ☎ 01422 316000
16 Town Hall Street, Sowerby Bridge, West Yorkshire HX6 2EA

R L d org F

The Magpie Café ☎ 01947 602058
14 Pier Road, Whitby, North Yorkshire YO21 3PU R L a

The Blake Head Bookshop & Vegetarian Café ☎ 01904 623767
104 Micklegate, York YO1 6JX
Lunches, breakfasts, coffees and cakes. All food home-made. Family friendly with disabled access. C L c

El Piano ☎ 01904 610676
15-17 Grape Lane, The Quarter, York YO1 7HU
Wholly vegan and gluten-free, right in the centre of York's original Quarter. Outside seating and function rooms. R L d org F

The Spurriergate Centre ☎ 01904 629393
St Michaels Church, Spurriergate, York YO1 9QR C a

North West England

Cheshire

Cafés, restaurants, pubs

Hullabaloo ☎ 0161 941 4288
5 Kings Court, 39-40 Railway Street, Altrincham WA14 2RD
R/C L a w org F

Francs Bistro ☎ 01244 317952
14 Cuppin Street, Chester CH1 2BN
R L a org F

Sokrates Greek Taverna ☎ 0161 282 0050
25A Northenden Road, Sale M33 2DH
R L a

Cumbria

Rothay Manor   ☎ 015394 33605, fax 015394 33607
Rothay Bridge, Ambleside LA22 0EH

email: hotel@rothaymanor.co.uk
website: www.rothaymanor.co.uk

Award-winning Country
House Hotel in the heart
of the Lake District.
Ideal for walking,
sightseeing or relaxing.
Renowned for the
warm, friendly
atmosphere; excellent
restaurant. Rooms and
suites for families and disabled
guests. Free use of nearby Leisure Centre. See also page 9.
H INS CatA L DA Ve NS Acc37

No 1 Guest House

☎ and fax 01228 547285

1 Etterby Street, Stanwix, Carlisle CA3 9JB

email: sheila@carlislebandb.co.uk
website: www.carlislebandb.co.uk

We are situated on the line of Hadrian's Wall and a 10-minute walk away from the Sands Centre, the Castle and Carlisle city centre. Not far from the M6 motorway, near the border with Scotland, yet only a short distance from the Lake District. Carlisle itself is steeped in ancient Roman and Reiver history. AA 4 Star rated. Evening meals must be booked ahead as we always cook fresh food bought on the day.
PH INS CatB Ve NS Acc5

Barf House Vegetarian/Vegan B&B

☎ 017687 76789

Dubwath, Bassenthwaite Lake, Cockermouth CA13 9YD

email: bob.pegasus@tiscali.co.uk
website: www.barfhouse.co.uk

100% vegetarian/vegan accommodation in peaceful location near the shore of Bassenthwaite Lake. Magnificent views across to the Skiddaw range. Excellent base for walking, cycling, sailing or just relaxing. Evening meals and special diets available on request. Car & cycle parking.
PH CatB V Ve NS Acc4

Lancrigg Vegetarian Country House Hotel

☎ 015394 35317

Easedale, Grasmere LA22 9QN

email: info@lancrigg.co.uk
website: www.lancrigg.co.uk

Peace and relaxation in historic country house with comfortable accommodation. Some rooms with whirlpool baths. International vegetarian cuisine. Special diets. Restaurant fully certified organic. Therapies and entry to  country health spa available. Stunning mountain setting with 30 acres private grounds.

H INS CatA L V Ve NS Acc26

Ardrig Vegetarian Bed and Breakfast

☎ 01539 736879

144 Windermere Road, Kendal LA9 5EZ

email: enquiry@ardrigvegetarian.com
website: www.ardrigvegetarian.com

Ardrig is a quiet, friendly home with clean comfortable rooms. Breakfast is vegetarian/vegan, fresh, filling, mostly Fairtrade, organic food. Kendal has restaurants, arts centre, cinemas, museums, shops and transport links to lakes and fells.

PH CatB V Ve NS Acc5

Nab Cottage

☎ 015394 35311, fax 015394 35493

Rydal, Ambleside LA22 9SD

email: tim@nabcottage.com
website: www.rydalwater.com

In the heart of the Lake
District, Nab Cottage is
beautifully situated
overlooking Rydal Water
and surrounded by
mountains. It dates from
the 16th century and has
many literary associations.
Cosy, informal atmosphere
- delicious home-cooked

food. Shiatsu, massage and Reiki available. See also page 9.
G INS CatB Ve NS Acc18

Sefton House

☎ 01229 582190

34 Queen Street, Ulverston LA12 7AF

email: reservations@seftonhouse.co.uk
website: www.seftonhouse.co.uk

Sefton House is a clean and
comfortable family-run guest house,
centrally located in the traditional
market town of Ulverston. Our
vegetarian breakfasts are freshly
prepared using locally-grown,
organic and Fairtrade ingredients
wherever possible. We cater for
special diets.
G INS CatB V Ve NS Acc11

St John's Lodge ☎ 015394 43078, fax 015394 88054
Lake Road, Windermere LA23 2EQ
email: mail@st-johns-lodge.co.uk
website: www.st-johns-lodge.co.uk
See display ad below.
G INS CatB Ve NS Acc24

Cafés, restaurants, pubs
Siskins Café ☎ 017687 78410
Whinlatter Visitor Centre, Braithwaite, Keswick CA12 5TW
C L a w org
The Watermill Café ☎ 016974 78267
Priests Mill, Caldbeck, Wigton CA7 8DR
C a F
Quince & Medlar Restaurant ☎ 01900 823579
11-13 Castlegate, Cockermouth CA13 9EU
R L c org
Villa Colombina ☎ 015394 35268
Grasmere LA22 9SH
R/C a

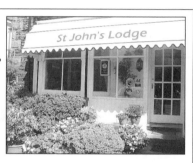

The Green Valley Organic Restaurant at Lancrigg ☎ 015394 35317
Easedale, Grasmere LA22 9QN
Fully organic. Healthy, delicious and nutritious. Special diets. All
ingredients certified 100% organic. Open every day. Breakfasts,
lunches, afternoon teas, evening meals. Stunning location, ½ mile
from Grasmere village. Website www.greenvalleyorganic.co.uk and
email purefood@greenvalleyorganic.co.uk   R/C c w org

The Quaker Tapestry Exhibition and Tearooms ☎ 01539 722975
Friends Meeting House, Stramongate, Kendal LA9 4BH
See display ad below.   C c w org F

Union Jack Café ☎ 01539 722458
15 Kirkland, Kendal LA9 7NF   C L a

Waterside Wholefoods Café/Restaurant & Shop ☎ 01539 733252
Kent View, Waterside, Kendal LA9 4DZ
See display ad on page 71.   C L c w org F

The Lakeland Pedlar Wholefood Café ☎ 017687 74492
Hendersons Yard, Bell Close, Keswick CA12 5JD
See display ad on page 71.   R/C L c w org F

Maysons Restaurant ☎ 017687 74104
   33 Lake Road, Keswick CA12 5DQ   R/C L a
Little Salkeld Watermill ☎ 01768 881523
   Little Salkeld, Penrith CA10 1NN
   See display ad above.   C c w org F
The Village Bakery ☎ 01768 881811
   Melmerby, nr Penrith CA10 1HE
   Café and bakeshop offering healthy wholesome meals and specialising
   in products suitable for people with special diet requirements. Open
   all year (excluding Christmas, New Year and first two weeks of
   January). Website www.village-bakery.com, email restaurant@village-
   bakery.com.   R/C L a w org F

Isle of Man

Fernleigh
☎ and fax 01624 842435

Marine Parade, Peel IM5 1PB

email: fernleigh@manx.net
website: www.isleofman.com/business/f/fernleigh

PEEL CASTLE

Looking across the bay, in the quiet fishing village of Peel. Join us in our comfortable Victorian home on the sea front, standard and en-suite rooms. Complemented by our excellent choice of home-made vegetarian and traditional breakfasts. Standard room £25.00, en-suite £30.00 p.p.p.n.
G INS CatB Ve NS Acc22

Cafés, restaurants, pubs

Greens Vegetarian Restaurant ☎ 01624 629129
  Steam Railway Station, Bank Hill, Douglas IM1 4LL   R/C L c

Lancashire, Greater Manchester and Merseyside

The Cameo
☎ 01253 626144, fax 01253 296048

30 Hornby Road, Blackpool FY1 4QG

email: enquiries@blackpool-cameo.com
website: www.blackpool-cameo.com

See display ad on page 74.
G INS CatC L Ve NS Acc20

Cafés, restaurants, pubs

Vfresh Café ☎ 01254 844555
35 King Street, Blackburn BB2 2DH
See display ad below.   C c

Red Triangle Café ☎ 01282 832319
160 St James Street, Burnley BB11 1NR
An informal daytime community café Tuesdays to Saturdays, and a
relaxed candlelit bistro for evening meals on Fridays and Saturdays.
Events individually catered by request.   R/C L c w org F

Jim's Café ☎ 01282 868828
19-21 New Market Street, Colne BB8 9BJ
Fresh seasonal food, using locally-sourced ingredients; served with
high quality, affordable wines, in a creative, sensual, Parisian café
environment.   R L c

Sokrates Greek Taverna ☎ 01204 692100
80-84 Winter Hey Lane, Horwich, Bolton BL6 7NZ   R L a

Aardvark Café ☎ 0151 709 0025
    Blackwell University Bookshop, University of Liverpool, Alsop
    Building, Brownlow Hill, Liverpool L3 5TX
    See display ad above.   C a org F
Everyman Bistro and Bars ☎ 0151 708 9545
    5-9 Hope Street, Liverpool L1 9BH
    See display ad on page 77.   R/C/P L a org F
The Piazza Café Bar ☎ 0151 707 3536
    Metropolitan Cathedral, Mount Pleasant, Liverpool L3 5TQ
    See display ad on page 77.   C L a org F
Aardvark Café ☎ 0161 273 8000
    Blackwell University Bookshop, The Precinct Centre, Oxford Road,
    Manchester M13 9RN   C a org F
Earth Café ☎ 0161 834 1996
    16-20 Turner Street, The Northern Quarter, Manchester M4 1DZ
    Award-winning café and juice bar, situated in Manchester's Northern
    Quarter, serving fresh, seasonal, home-made ethical food and drinks.
                                          C c w org F

8th Day Vegetarian Health Food Shop and Café ☎ 0161 273 1850
111 Oxford Road, Manchester M1 7DU
Pots of freshly made soups, salads and stews, lots of organic fruit and
veg and 300+ Fairtrade lines – just for starters!   C L(shop) c w org F
The Greenhouse ☎ 0161 224 0730
331 Great Western Street, Rusholme, Manchester M14 4AN
R L c w org F
duk ☎ 01772 202220
16-18 Lancaster Road, Preston PR1 1DA
Award-winning bespoke world tapas brought to you by the famous
duk squad. Also now at Pond.   R L a F
Pond Restaurant ☎ 01772 824988
37 Cannon Street, Preston PR1 3NT   R L a F

Wales

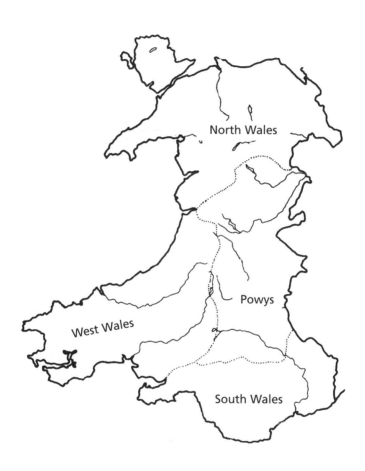

North Wales

Powys

West Wales

South Wales

North Wales

Ivy House

☎ 01341 422535, fax 01341 422689

Finsbury Square, Dolgellau, Gwynedd LL40 1RF

email: marg.bamford@btconnect.com
website: www.ivyhouse-dolgellau.co.uk

Country town guest house offering attractive accommodation, good food and a welcoming atmosphere. The six bedrooms have TV, hairdryers and tea/coffee facilities, four of them have en-suite facilities. Delicious vegetarian/traditional breakfasts. Open all year.
G INS CatB Ve NS Acc13

Snowdonia

Exclusively vegetarian/vegan hotel in three acres of private gardens. Spectacular views over the river estuary towards Portmeirion, the sea and the mountains. Excellent home cooking with many products from our organic fruit/vegetable garden.

No smoking throughout. Licensed for a selection of organic wines and beers. Relax in our peaceful and friendly environment.

Easy access to beaches, mountains, historic Welsh and English castles, steam trains, slate and copper mines and Portmeirion – the world famous Italianate village.

Tremeifion Vegetarian Hotel

Soar Road, Talsarnau, nr Harlech, Gwynedd LL47 6UH
Tel 01766 770491   E-mail: enquire@tremeifionvegetarianhotel.co.uk
Website: www.tremeifionvegetarianhotel.co.uk

Tremeifion Vegetarian Hotel ☎ 01766 770491
Soar Road, Talsarnau, nr Harlech, Gwynedd LL47 6UH

email: enquire@tremeifionvegetarianhotel.co.uk
website: www.tremeifionvegetarianhotel.co.uk

See display ad on page 80.
H CatA L V Ve NS CN Acc10

Cafés, restaurants, pubs
Alpine Coffee Shop and Gallery ☎ 01690 710747
Station Road, Betws-y-Coed, Conwy LL24 0AE
The menu includes a mixture of food: vegetarian, vegan, gluten- and
dairy-free products. We also specialise in loose tea and good coffee.   C a F

Kyffin ☎ 01248 355161
129 High Street, Bangor, Gwynedd LL57 1NT
See display ad on page 81.   C c w org F

Beddgelert Tearooms & Bistro ☎ 01766 890543
Waterloo House, Beddgelert, Gwynedd LL55 4UY   R/C L a

Powys

Trericket Mill Vegetarian Guest House, Bunkhouse & Camping ☎ 01982 560312
Erwood, Builth Wells LD2 3TQ

email: mail@trericket.co.uk
website: www.trericket.co.uk

We offer a range of
accommodation
overlooking the River
Wye, from camping and
bunkroom, with
optional bedding and
breakfast, to en-suite
bed and wholesome
vegetarian breakfast in
our grade 2* listed corn
mill and cosy
bunkhouse set in an old
cider orchard beside the
mill stream. Small but
friendly! Contact Nicky or Alistair Legge.
G INS CatB V Ve NS Acc16+camping

Elan Valley Hotel ☎ 01597 810448, fax 01597 810824
Elan Valley, nr Rhayader LD6 5HN

email: info@elanvalleyhotel.co.uk
website: www.elanvalleyhotel.co.uk

See display ad on page 82 and also page 11.
H INS CatA L DA Ve NS Acc20+

Primrose Earth Centre

☎ 01497 847636

Primrose Farm, Felindre, Brecon LD3 0ST

email: jan.benham@ukonline.co.uk
website: www.primroseearthcentre.co.uk

Organic fruit and vegetable smallholding at the foot of the Black Mountains; on national cycle route; near Hay-on-Wye. Guests prepare own breakfast, we provide fresh ingredients. B&B, evening meals on request; quiet retreats for de-stressing from busy lives; sound healing courses available.
PH CatC V Ve NS CN Acc5

The Old Post Office

☎ 01497 820008

Llanigon, Hay-on-Wye HR3 5QA

website: www.oldpost-office.co.uk

See display ad on page 85.
G CatB V Ve NS CN Acc6

Maenllwyd Guest House

☎ and fax 01654 702928

Newtown Road, Machynlleth SY20 8EY

email: maenllwyd@btinternet.com
website: www.meanllwyd.co.uk

We are within walking distance of all amenities and offer a warm welcome to all our guests. Maenllwyd is situated approximately 4 miles from the Centre for Alternative Technology and is also on the Glyndwr National Trail and Sustrans Route 8. For further information please visit our website.
G INS CatB NS Acc16

The Old Post Office

Llanigon, **Hay-on-Wye** HR3 5QA
Tel 01497 820008
website: www.oldpost-office.co.uk
Exclusively vegetarian

A very special find at the foot of the Black Mountains and **only two miles from the famous second-hand book town of Hay-on-Wye.**

Charming 17th-century house with beams and oak floor boards. Lovely walks and views of the Wye Valley and Black Mountains. Dogs by arrangement. *Rough Guide, Lonely Planet,* Alastair Sawday's *Special Places to Stay* and *Which?* recommended.

We also have a Georgian cottage in Hay-on-Wye available as holiday let or B&B (self-serve continental breakfast).

Please visit our website for more information.

Cafés, restaurants, pubs

The Restaurant at the Elan Valley Hotel ☎ 01597 810448
Elan Valley, near Rhayader LD6 5HN   R L a
The Quarry Café ☎ 01654 702624
13a Maengwyn Street, Machynlleth SY20 8EB   C c w org F
The Hat Shop Restaurant ☎ 01544 260017
7 High Street, Presteigne LD8 2BA   R L a w org F
Old Swan Tea Rooms ☎ 01597 811060
West Street, Rhayader LD6 5AB   C a

South Wales

Awen Vegetarian B&B and Dining

☎ 01495 244615

Penrhiwgwair Cottage, Twyn Road, Abercarn, Newport, Gwent NP11 5AS

email: info@awenbandb.com
website: www.awenbandb.com

Our award-winning, exclusively vegetarian, environmentally-friendly B&B now offers seasonal organic dining. This historic 16th-century cottage has a romantic four-poster bed and many original features. Breathtaking scenery and mountain walks outside the front door. Vegan and special diets welcomed. See also page 11.
G CatB V Ve NS Acc6

The Nurtons

☎ 01291 689253

Tintern, near Chepstow, Monmouthshire NP16 7NX

email: info@thenurtons.co.uk
website: www.thenurtons.co.uk

A historic house on an ancient site, secluded in its own 30 acres, with stunning views of the Wye Valley. We have a long-established reputation for our excellent and generous vegetarian cuisine; very largely organic, seasonally home-grown. B&B in comfortable en-suite accommodation, evening meals by arrangement, retreats for small groups welcome. See also page 11.
PH INS CatB V Ve NS Acc12

Cafés, restaurants, pubs

Hunky Dory Bistro ☎ 01633 257850
17 Charles Street, Newport, Gwent NP20 1JU   C c
Crumbs ☎ 02920 395007
33 Morgan Arcade, Cardiff, South Glamorgan CF10 1AF
DO YOUR BODY A FAVOUR – EAT 'CRUMBS'! Established 1970
by present proprietor Judi. Home-made salads and hot food. All
veggie – some vegan, wheat- and dairy-free.   R c
Embassy Café ☎ 02920 373144
Cathays Community Centre, 36 Cathays Terrace, Cardiff, South
Glamorgan CF24 4HX   C c w org F
Vegetarian Food Studio ☎ 02920 238222
109 Penarth Road, Cardiff, South Glamorgan CF11 8AB   C c
Govinda's Vegetarian Restaurant ☎ 01792 468469
8 Cradock Street, Swansea, West Glamorgan SA1 3EN   R c

West Wales

Pen Pynfarch   ☎ 01559 384948
Llandysul, Carmarthenshire SA44 4RU

email: enquiries@penpynfarch.co.uk
website: www.penpynfarch.co.uk

Pen Pynfarch, course centre and
holiday retreat, lies at the head of
a steeply wooded valley in South
West Wales. For groups of 5-12
we offer vegetarian full board and
accommodation, with the use of
a warm, light studio. For holiday
stays there is a cosy self-catering
cottage and a simple studio flat.
See also page 10.

Full board guesthouse £60 pppn/self-catering V Ve NS CN Acc12

Over the Rainbow

☎ 01239 811155

Plas Tyllwyd, Tan-y-groes, near Cardigan, Ceredigion SA43 2JD

email: info@overtherainbowwales.co.uk
website: www.overtherainbowwales.co.uk

West Wales vegetarian guest house. This 18th-century Georgian mansion is a haven of rural seclusion in 18 acres of woodland and gardens. Stay B&B or hire exclusively for small group holidays, residential courses and workshops. Well-appointed, sumptuous, centrally-heated rooms. Here you can unwind and relax watching the stars and listening to the silence. See also page 10.
G CatB V Ve NS CN Acc9

Cuffern Manor

☎ 01437 710071

Roch, Haverfordwest, Pembrokeshire SA62 6HB

email: enquiries@cuffernmanor.co.uk
website: www.cuffernmanor.co.uk

Our eighteenth-century Manor House in the spectacular Pembrokeshire countryside is adjacent to the stunning Pembrokeshire Coast National Park near Newgale Beach. Wifi access. Lift and accessible shower/toilet. Quality organic, fair-traded food or local produce. Delicious vegetarian and vegan food. Winner of Pembrokeshire Produce 2006 Award for 'Best use of local food'. See also page 11.
G INS CatB DA Ve NS CN Acc20

Cafés, restaurants, pubs

Waverley Stores & Restaurant ☎ 01267 236521
23 Lammas Street, Carmarthen, Carmarthenshire SA31 3AL
R L c w org F

The Hive on the Quay ☎ 01545 570445
Cadwgan Place, Aberaeron, Ceredigion SA46 0BU
Bustling harbourside café serving local seafood, soups and salads and sandwiches, ciders and wine, lots of cakes and, our speciality, honey ice creams.
R/C L a

The Treehouse ☎ 01970 615791
14 Stryd y Popty/Baker Street, Aberystwyth, Ceredigion SY23 2BY
Aberystwyth's favourite café and shop for the best organic, local and seasonal produce. Vegans, vegetarians, carnivores and free-thinkers all welcome.
R L a w org F

The Mulberry Bush ☎ 01570 423317
2 Bridge Street, Lampeter, Ceredigion SA48 7HG
Outstanding vegetarian/vegan wholefood store and café with organic salad and juice bar. Fully licensed. Monthly restaurant nights with live music.
R/C L c w org F

Morgan's ☎ 01437 720508
20 Nun Street, St Davids, Pembrokeshire SA62 6NT
R L a F

Scotland

Orkney and Shetland Islands (NE of the Scottish mainland, here shown at half scale of main map)

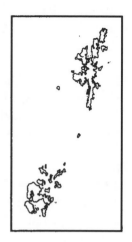

Western Scottish Islands

Scottish Highlands

Aberdeenshire and Moray

Angus, Perth and Kinross

Argyll

Fife

Central Scotland

Lothian

Ayrshire

Borders

Dumfries and Galloway

Aberdeenshire & Moray

Fournet Guest House ☎ 01340 821428
Balvenie Street, Dufftown, Moray AB55 4AB

email: alison@woosnam8488.freeserve.co.uk
website: www.noahsarkbistro.co.uk

Fournet House provides a haven in the hills in Dufftown in North East Scotland for 'Wellbeing at its Best'. Located halfway between the beautiful scenic coast and the Braes of Glenlivet and the Cabrach, it is easily accessible from either Inverness or Aberdeen airports. Come by train

to Huntly or Keith station or bring your own car! On offer is outrageously comfortable accommodation en-suite and one bedroom has its own foaming whirlpool bath. Feel at home in the lovely reception room. There is a variety of things to do and delicious and innovative food to enjoy. The wellbeing and therapy garden is being developed at the back of the house. Choose from a collection of packages or simply taste the experience in an overnight stay. Please watch the website for more details. See also page 12.
G CatB L DA Ve NS Acc8

Cafés, restaurants, pubs

Noah's Ark Whole Food Café and Licensed Bistro ☎ 01340 821428
Fournet House, Balvenie Street, Dufftown, Moray AB55 4AB
Fun, funky and irrepressible! The handmade, whole food cuisine is served from breakfast through to delicious dinner. Noah's Ark offers a wide nutritional rainbow on a plate, including its own home-grown vegetables complementing the locally sourced produce.   R/C L a w

Argyll

Cafés, restaurants, pubs

The Smiddy Bistro ☎ 01546 603606
Smithy Lane, Lochgilphead PA31 8TA   R L a

Ayrshire

Drumskeoch Farm B&B   ☎ 01465 841172

Pinwherry, nr Girvan KA26 0QB

email: drumskeoch@wildmail.com
website: www.drumskeoch.co.uk

Unique family-run green, organic
vegetarian/vegan B&B in naturally
renovated rural farmhouse, with own
water source and beautiful views of the
surrounding hills. Comfortable and
relaxed atmosphere, delicious home-
cooked food, and a great base for
walking, sightseeing or relaxing.
PH CatA V Ve NS CN Acc4

Borders

Cafés, restaurants, pubs

Tibbie Shiels Inn ☎ 01750 42231
St Mary's Loch, Selkirkshire, Scottish Borders TD7 5LH
This historic coaching inn is located 16 miles from Selkirk, on the
A708 to Moffat. Tibbie Shiels serves a variety of food daily 12-8pm,
all produce is sourced locally where possible or grown on site.
R/P L a

Dumfries and Galloway

Cafés, restaurants, pubs

Abbey Cottage ☎ 01387 850377
26 Main Street, New Abbey, Dumfries DG2 8BY
Situated beside historical Sweetheart Abbey, we serve morning coffee,
light lunches and afternoon tea, baked or cooked on our premises.
Also gift shop stocking preserves and crafts from around the region.
www.abbeycottagetearoom.com   R a org F

Edinburgh

Ardgarth Guest House

☎ 0131 669 3021, fax 0131 468 1221
1 St Mary's Place, Portobello, Edinburgh EH15 2QF

email: stay@ardgarth.com
website: www.ardgarth.com

Tastefully adapted from a
large Victorian home, in a
wide, quiet street with easy
parking. City centre 20
minutes by bus, short stroll
to sandy beach and a
promenade that is the envy
of Edinburgh! Single,
double, twin and family
rooms, some en-suite.
Cots/high chairs available.

Ground floor rooms fully equipped for disabled people.
G INS CatB L DA Ve NS Acc21

Six Mary's Place

A welcoming guest house situated in the Stockbridge area of Edinburgh – a quiet location only 10 minutes away from the city centre. Free Wi-Fi throughout the building as well as complementary tea and coffee.

Home-made vegetarian breakfast served in the conservatory overlooking our private garden. Use of kitchen facilities for guests staying in the family room (max 6 people sharing).

Tel: 0131 332 8965

Six Mary's Place, Raeburn Place, Stockbridge, Edinburgh. EH4 1JH

info@sixmarysplace.co.uk
www.sixmarysplace.co.uk

Elmview
☎ 0131 228 1973

15 Glengyle Terace, Edinburgh EH3 9LN

email: nici@elmview.co.uk
website: www.elmview.co.uk

Robin and Nici Hill's elegant and peaceful accommodation is situated in the heart of Edinburgh, only 15 minutes' walk from Princes Street and Edinburgh Castle. Totally non-smoking and graded 5 Stars by the AA.
G INS CatA Ve NS Acc8

Six Mary's Place Guest House

☎ 0131 332 8965, fax 0131 624 7060

Raeburn Place, Stockbridge, Edinburgh EH4 1JH

email: info@sixmarysplace.co.uk
website: www.sixmarysplace.co.uk

See display ad on page 94.

G INS CatA Ve NS Acc23

The Walton ☎ 0131 556 1137, fax 0131 557 8367

79 Dundas Street, Edinburgh EH3 6SD

email: enquiries@waltonhotel.com
website: www.waltonhotel.com

The Walton is a 4 Star guest house situated in Edinburgh's historic New Town. Close to restaurants, tourist attractions and boutique shops, The Walton is an excellent choice of accommodation for your trip to Edinburgh.

G INS CatA NS Acc24

Cafés, restaurants, pubs

The Baked Potato Shop ☎ 0131 225 7572
56 Cockburn Street, Edinburgh EH1 1PB
Extensive selection of vegetarian/vegan fillings, plus vegan cakes
home made. Open 7 days 9am-9pm. Take-away c

David Bann Restaurant ☎ 0131 556 5888
56-58 St Mary's Street, Edinburgh EH1 1SX R L c

The Engine Shed ☎ 0131 662 0040
19 St Leonard's Lane, Edinburgh EH8 9SD
See display ad on page 96. C c w org F

Filmhouse Café Bar ☎ 0131 229 5932
88 Lothian Road, Edinburgh EH3 9BZ C L a org F

Henderson's Bistro ☎ 0131 225 2605
25c Thistle Street, Edinburgh EH2 1DX
Elegant, intimate yet relaxed, the Bistro offers a tempting range of international vegetarian flavours. Open seven days from noon. Email mail@hendersonsofedinburgh.co.uk, website
www.hendersonsofedinburgh.co.uk. R L c w org F

Henderson's @ St John's ☎ 0131 229 0212
3 Lothian Road, Edinburgh EH1 2EP
This café, situated in atmospheric barrel-vaulted surroundings in Edinburgh's West End, boasts a garden terrace for al fresco dining. Open every day. Website www.hendersonsofedinburgh.co.uk

C L c w org F

Henderson's Restaurant ☎ 0131 225 2131
94 Hanover Street, Edinburgh EH2 1DR
Scotland's legendary vegetarian restaurant, offering delicious, wholesome food, nightly live music and fabulous contemporary art in the Janet Henderson Gallery. 8 til late Monday-Saturday. Email mail@hendersonsofedinburgh.co.uk, website www.hendersonsofedinburgh.co.uk.

R L c w org F

Viva Mexico ☎ 0131 226 5145
41 Cockburn Street, Edinburgh EH1 1BS

R L a

Glasgow and Central Scotland

Adelaide's

☎ 0141 248 4970, fax 0141 226 4247

209 Bath Street, Glasgow G2 4HZ

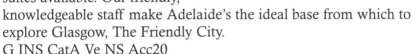

email: reservations@adelaides.co.uk
website: www.adelaides.co.uk

Highly acclaimed Guest House situated
in award-winning listed building with
family/twin/double and single en-
suites available. Our friendly,
knowledgeable staff make Adelaide's the ideal base from which to
explore Glasgow, The Friendly City.
G INS CatA Ve NS Acc20

Cafés, restaurants, pubs

mono ☎ 0141 553 2400
12 Kings Court, King Street, Glasgow G1 5RB
Exciting café/bar in Glasgow's Merchant City. All our tasty food is

animal-free. Site includes microbrewery/venue/gallery/record shop.
Website www.monocafebar.com. See display ad on page 97.

C/P L d w org

STEREO ☎ 0141 222 2254
20-28 Renfield Lane, Glasgow G2 6PH
City centre café/bar near Central Station. Breads, pies, cakes baked
on premises. Healthy sit-in or take-away. Delicious salads and coffee.
Website www.stereocafebar.com. See display ad above.

C/P L d w org

Tapa Bakehouse ☎ 0141 554 9981
21 Whitehill Street, Dennistoun, Glasgow G31 2LH   C c w org F
Tapa Coffeehouse ☎ 0141 423 9494
721 Pollokshaws Road, Glasgow G41 2AA   C a w org F
The 78 ☎ 0141 576 5018
14 Kelvinhaugh Street, Glasgow G3 8NU
Delightful pub in west end of Glasgow serving delicious and healthy
animal-free food. Organic drinks, real fire, 1927 gramophone! Website
www.the78cafebar.com. See display ad on page 99.   C/P L d w org

The Scottish Highlands

Nevis View
☎ 01397 772447, fax 01397 772800

14 Farrow Drive, Corpach, Fort William, Inverness-shire PH33 7JW

email: enquiries@nevisviewfortwilliam.co.uk
website: www.nevisviewfortwilliam.co.uk

A warm welcome awaits you at 'Nevis View'. We are vegetarians who can cater for vegans and meat-eaters too. The house is of unusual design and lies on a small award-winning estate of architect-designed houses, 4.5 miles from Fort William.
PH CatC Ve NS Acc6

Creag Meagaidh B&B

☎ 01540 673798, fax 0870 838 1101

Main Street, Newtonmore, Inverness-shire PH20 1DP

email: creag-meagaidh@live.co.uk
website: www.creag-meagaidh.co.uk

Luxurious B&B within Cairngorm National Park. Mountains, lochs and rivers all within walking distance. Home-made bread and jams, Fairtrade tea and coffee. Full board available for groups/longer stays. Vegetarian owners. Close to train and bus stops. See also page 11.
PH INS CatB Ve NS Acc6

Cuildorag House

☎ 01855 821529

Onich, nr Fort William, Inverness-shire PH33 6SD

email: enquiries@cuildoraghouse.com
website: www.cuildoraghouse.com

Stay and relax in our comfortable Victorian house set amongst spectacular lochs and mountains. Large delicious breakfasts and evening meals (often organic and from the garden). Days walking, mountain biking, touring, exploring Ben Nevis, Glencoe, Ardnamurchan, castles, steam trains …
PH CatB V Ve NS Acc6

Cafés, restaurants, pubs

Cawdor Castle ☎ 01667 404401
Nairn, Inverness-shire IV12 5RD
R L a org F (open 1st May to 2nd Sunday in October)
Station Tea Room ☎ 01349 865894
Station Square, Dingwall, Ross-shire IV15 9JX   C a
The Ceilidh Place ☎ 01854 612103
14 West Argyle Street, Ullapool, Ross-shire IV26 2TY
R/C/P L a w org F
Loch Croispol Bookshop, Restaurant & Gallery ☎ 01971 511777
2 Balnakeil, Durness, by Lairg, Sutherland IV27 4PT   R a

Shetland Islands

Cafés, restaurants, pubs

Da Böd Café ☎ 01806 503348
Hillswick Wildlife Sanctuary, Hillswick
ZE2 9RW
We serve vegetarian and vegan food in a
400-year-old building at weekends during
May to September from 11am, please
phone to book an evening meal. Payment
by donation. Also B&B for 2 people in a
lovely room with sea views. All proceeds
go to Hillswick Wildlife Sanctuary, a seal
and otter sanctuary.
C c w org

The Western Scottish Islands

The Old Croft House Vegetarian B&B

☎ 01470 532375

6 Carbost, Skeabost Bridge, by Portree, Isle of Skye IV51 9PD

email: samcrowe@tiscali.co.uk
website: www.vegetarianskye.co.uk

Come for a relaxing stay in our beautiful 19th-century croft house. We aim to provide a B&B experience that is a bit special, with stunning views, breakfasts that are truly indulgent and great hosts, who will really look after you.
PH CatB V Ve NS Acc2+child

Foxwood

Foxwood is surrounded by inspirational countryside, standing in 4 acres of land with sea and mountain views. The sunrises and sunsets can be unbelievable.

Spacious en-suites, and single room.

Sauna, jacuzzi, steam cabinet and alternative therapies are available.

Ideal for touring, walking, cycling, relaxing.

11a Ullinish by Struan, Isle of Skye IV56 8FD

e-mail treefox@hotmail.com
website www.scotland–info.co.uk/foxwood

Foxwood

☎ 01470 572331

11A Ullinish by Struan, Isle of Skye IV56 8FD

email: treefox@hotmail.com

website: www.scotland-info.co.uk/foxwood

See display ad on page 102.

G CatB DA V Ve NS CN Acc6

Further vegetarian information

For users of this guide who would like further information on vegetarianism or veganism in Britain, or information on a particular area, we list below a number of organisations, groups and information centres. When writing, please include a stamp for return postage.

National

Friends Vegetarian Society
9 Astons Close, Woods Lane, Amblecote, nr Stourbridge, West Midlands DY5 2QT, tel 01384 423899

Jewish Vegetarian Society
855 Finchley Road, London NW11 8LX, tel 020 8455 0692

Muslim Vegan/Vegetarian Society
59 Bray Towers, 136 Adelaide Road, London NW3 3JU, tel 020 7483 1742 Run by Rafeeque Ahmed, the author of a booklet called 'Islam and Vegetarianism'.

The Vegetarian Society (UK) Ltd.
Parkdale, Dunham Road, Altrincham, Cheshire WA14 4QG, tel 0161 925 2000, fax 0161 926 9182

The Vegan Society Ltd.
21 Hylton Street, Hockley, Birmingham B18 6HJ, tel 0845 458 8244/0121 523 1730

Viva! (Vegetarians International Voice for Animals)
8 York Court, Wilder Street, Bristol BS2 8QH, tel 0845 456 8220, fax 0845 456 8230 Viva! campaigns to stop cruelty to animals and to promote a vegetarian/vegan lifestyle.

Young Indian Vegetarians
226 London Road, West Croydon, Surrey CR0 2TF, email animalahimsa@yahoo.co.uk

England (by county)

Thames Valley Vegans & Vegetarians
68 Peppard Road, Emmer Green, Reading, Berkshire RG4 8TL, tel 0118 946 4858, email t3v@makessense.co.uk

Chiltern Veggies
tel 01628 773555, email chilternveggies@yahoo.co.uk

Milton Keynes Vegetarians, Vegans and Animal Rights
13 Peers Lane, Shenley Church End, Milton Keynes, Buckinghamshire MK5 6BG, tel 01908 503919, email mkvegan475@talktalk.net

Chester & Clwyd Vegetarian Group
Nant Yr Hafod Cottage, Hafod Bilston, Llandegla, Clwyd LL11 3BG, tel 01978 790442, email indesigneko@aol.com

Chester Vegetarians and Vegans
tel 07962 385213, email chesterveg@hotmail.co.uk

Wirral Vegetarian/Vegan Group
103 Bermuda Road, Moreton, Wirral, Cheshire CH46 6AU, tel 0151 678 1487, email info@wirralveggies.org.uk

Tees Valley Veggies & Vegans
3 Church Lane, Marske by the Sea, Redcar, Cleveland TS11 7LJ, tel 07950 017928, email tees_veg@yahoo.co.uk

Cornwall Veggies
19c Well Lane, Church Street, Falmouth, Cornwall TR11 3EG, tel 01326 317583, email pinnersohmigod2000@yahoo.co.uk

Lakeland Living Veg Group
5 Bridge Street Close, Cockermouth, Cumbria CA13 9RR, tel 01900 824045, email veggielakelandliving@tiscali.co.uk

Amber Valley Vegetarians & Vegans (Derbyshire)
tel 01773 833294, email amberveg@hotmail.co.uk

Derby Vegetarian Society
P.O. Box 41, Derby DE1 9ZR, tel 0871 855 3912, email manjit01@ntlworld.com

Derbyshire Vegetarians
tel 01298 72472

Dartveggie (Dartmouth, Devon, area)
email dartveggie@hotmail.co.uk

Exeter Vision Info Centre
1 Romsey Drive, Exeter, Devon EX2 4PB, tel 01392 273694, email pace09@virginmedia.com

North & Mid Devon Vegetarian Info Centre
Fern Tor, Meshaw, South Molton, Devon EX36 4NA, tel 01769 550339, email veg@ferntor.co.uk

Plymouth Environment Centre
Greenbank Neighbourhood Office, 35 Armada Street, Plymouth, Devon PL4
8LZ, tel 01752 290015, email info@plymouthenvironmentcentre.org.uk (Chris Deacon)

Dorset Vegans
tel 01202 824783, email jjnanaz@yahoo.co.uk

Barking Vegetarian Info Centre
288 Howard Road, Barking, Essex IG11 7DN, tel 020 8252 5846 evenings

North East Essex Vegans
tel 01379 687293, email ApWFh@aol.com

Southend Animal Aid
PO Box 211, Short Street, Southend on Sea, Essex SS1 1AA, tel 01268 756026, email southendanimalaid@hotmail.com

Southend Area Veggies Information Centre (Essex)
tel 01702 540903, email soocoleman4@aol.com

VegSX
4 Tyrrells Road, Billericay, Essex CM11 2QE, tel 07970 732668, email veganessex@hotmail.com

Manchester Vegan Society
69 Lonsdale Road, Heaton, Bolton BL1 4PW, tel 07980 161025. email sarahalliez@yahoo.co.uk, website www.manchester.vegangroup.co.uk

Manchester Vegetarian & Vegan Group
550 St Helens Road, Bolton BL3 3SJ, tel 01204 654401, email mike@mvvg.co.uk

Stockport Vegetarians and Vegans (Greater Manchester)
tel 0161 217 9094, email antonybyatt@hotmail.com

Vegetarian Information
100 Sarah Robinson House, Queen Street, Portsmouth, Hampshire PO1 3JA, email michael.maybury2@ntlworld.com

Wye Valley Veggies
6 Bearcroft, Weobley, Herefordshire HR4 8TA, tel 01432 277493, email info@w-v-v.org.uk

North Herts Vegetarians and Vegans
4 Oaktree Close, Letchworth Garden City, Hertfordshire SG6 3XY, tel 01462 643424, email info@nhvegetariansandvegans.org.uk

Isle of Wight Vegetarians
Keepers Lock, Youngwood Way, Alverstone Garden Village, Sandown, Isle of Wight PO36 0HF, tel 01983 407098, email johnvl@tiscali.co.uk

Canterbury & Coastal Information Centre
83 Cherry Gardens, Herne Bay, Kent CT6 5QY, tel 01227 375661

Medway Veggies & Vegans
7 Masefield Drive, Cliffe Woods, Rochester, Kent ME3 8JW, tel 01634 294865, email sheilamccrossan@hotmal.com

North Kent Vegetarian Info Centre
Sycamore Lodge, 71 Barton Hill Drive, Minster on Sea, Sheerness, Kent ME12 3NF, tel 01795 873987

Sevenoaks Vegetarians, Vegans and Fellow Travellers
Westmount, Orchard Road, Pratts Bottom, Orpington, Kent BR6 7NT, tel 01689 859716, email lionden1@btinternet.com

Tunbridge Wells Vegan & Vegetarian Group (Kent)
Fletchers Cottage, Knowle Lane, Halland, East Sussex BN8 6PR, tel 01825 841104, email mark.hanna@virgin.net

Natural Healing
86 Queen Street, Great Harwood, Lancashire BB6 7AL, tel 01254 882233 (Elaine Aspin)

Lancs Veg
tel 01772 787163, email jj.dave@virgin.net

Wellbeing Workshops Veg Info Centre
Green Cottage, 514 Halliwell Road, St Paul's Conservation, Bolton, Lancashire BL1 8BP, tel 07050 256916, email alwynne@wellbeingworkshopsworldwide.com

Leicestershire Vegetarian and Vegan Group
Beeches, Smeeton Road, Saddington, Leicestershire LE8 0QT, tel 07786 175445, email leicesterveggies@1sd.co.uk

Boston Vegetarian Info Centre
23 Vauxhall Road, Boston, Lincolnshire PE21 0JB, tel 01205 350056, email john.richards2@virgin.net

Grantham VegSoc
3 Lindisfarne Way, Barrowby Lodge, Grantham, Lincolnshire NG31 8ST, tel 07988 724773, email granthamvegsoc@hotmail.co.uk

Grimsby Vegetarians
Flat 3, 6 Regent Gardens, Grimsby, Lincolnshire DN34 5AT, tel 01472

870738, email
gy.vegetarians@btinternet.com

Louth Vegetarian Group
37 Church Lane, Manby, Lincolnshire
LN11 8HL, tel 01507 327687, email
info@louthveggiegroup.org.uk

Vegan Lincs
18 Wolsey Way, Glebe Park, Lincoln
LN2 4QH, tel 01522 851915, email
linda.wardale@bluebottle.com

Ealing Veggie Group (London)
email ealingvegs@yahoo.co.uk

Greenwich Veggie Social Group
102 Blaker Court, Fairlawn, Charlton,
London SE7 7ET, tel 020 8856 2450,
email cotay47@yahoo.co.uk

Heavymetalveg (London)
email fabianafaria@ymail.com

Lesbian Vegans (London)
email tiger@tiger3.plus.com

North West London Vegetarian Group
3 St David Close, Cowley UB8 3SE, tel
01895 441881, email
chetna_jayjit@yahoo.com

South West London Veg Info Centre
Flat 424, Brandenburgh House, 116
Fulham Palace Road, London W6
9HH, tel 020 8741 6793, email
swveg1@yahoo.co.uk

VEG-London
email veg@veglondon.org

Merseyside Vegetarian Helplink
38 Hyacinth Close, Haydock, St
Helens, Merseyside WA11 0NZ, tel
01942 271761, email
marg4646@hotmail.com

ScouseVeg (Merseyside)
tel 0151 933 1338, email

jane@vegsoc.org

Harrow Vegetarian Society
152 Kenton Road, Harrow, Middlesex
HA3 8AZ, tel 020 8907 1235, email
kjoshi@pradipsweet.co.uk

Norfolk Vegetarian & Vegan Society
13 Ipswich Grove, Norwich, Norfolk
NR2 2LU, tel 01603 620784, email
aliciahowell@btinternet.com

Norwich Vegetarian Info Centre
email go-veg@fsmail.net

Northants Veggies
106 Eastfield Road, Wellingborough,
Northamptonshire NN8 1PS, tel 01933
381731, email
jane.mills7@ntlworld.com

Nottingham Vegetarian & Vegan Society
245 Gladstone Street, Nottingham
NG7 6HX, tel 0845 458 9595, email
nvvs@veggies.org.uk

OxVeg
20 Alden Crescent, Oxford OX3 9LT,
tel 01865 765580, email
ov@oxveg.co.uk

Oswestry Vegetarian Information Centre
Hobnob House, Maesbury Marsh,
Oswestry, Shropshire SY10 8JH, tel
01691 670404, email
webmaster@ivu.org

Shropshire Veggies & Vegans
1 Lees Farm Drive, Madeley, Telford,
Shropshire TF7 5SU, tel 01952 588878,
email david.whalley@talk21.com

North Somerset Vegetarian & Vegan Info
Centre
tel 01934 843853, email
rogerhards@venusmead.go-plus.net

Lichfield District Vegetarian Info Centre

29 Spring Road, Lichfield, Staffordshire WS13 6BJ, tel 07852 190855, email veggie@talktalk.net

Animals in Need Woking
7 Candlerush Close, Maybury, Woking, Surrey GU22 8AT, tel 01483 871392, email david.rainford4@ntlworld.com

Croydon Vegetarian Group
Flat 23, Zodiac Court, 165 London Road, Croydon, Surrey CR0 2RJ, tel 020 8688 6325

Guildford Vegetarian Society (Surrey)
tel 01483 425040

Kingston & Richmond Vegetarians
87 Porchester Road, Kingston-upon-Thames, Surrey KT1 3PW, tel 020 8541 3437, email walker@martinlake.plus.com

Twickenham & Surrey Vegetarian & Vegan Group
tel 01372 844368, email twsurreyveg@mailbolt.com

Woking Veggie & Vegan Group (Surrey)
wokingveg@aol.com

Brighton Area Veg*ans Info Centre
83 Sutton Road, Seaford, East Sussex BN25 4QH, tel 01323 896244, email angie@angiewright.co.uk

Lewes & Hastings Area Vegetarian & Vegan Group
Sandhills Oast, Bodle Street, nr Hailsham, East Sussex BN27 4QU, tel 01435 830150, email JLJDRJ@aol.com

Reddy Veg
39 Sallyport Crescent, Newcastle upon Tyne, Tyne & Wear NE1 2NE, tel 0191 285 9980, email

MikeCasselden@blueyonder.co.uk

VegNE
c/o Alternative Soles, 2 Alnwick Terrace, Wideopen, Newcastle upon Tyne, Tyne & Wear, tel 0191 236 4904, email mark@alternativesoles.com

Birmingham Vegetarians & Vegans
54-57 Allison Street, Digbeth, Birmingham, West Midlands B5 5TH, tel 0121 353 2442, email info@bvv.org.uk

Wolverhampton Veggies & Vegans
102 Shaw Road, Blakenhall, Wolverhampton, West Midlands WV2 3EP, tel 01902 451195

Wolves Veggies Info Centre
73 Oak Street, Merridale, Wolverhampton, West Midlands WV3 0AH, tel 01902 682550, email wolvesveggies@yahoo.co.uk

Swindon Veggies & Animal Concern (Wiltshire)
tel 01793 644796, email denisvegan01@tiscali.co.uk

Redditch Vegetarians & Vegans
PO Box 10202, Redditch, Worcestershire B98 8YT, tel 01527 458395, email reddiveggie@lycos.com

Leeds Vegetarian Society (West Yorkshire)
tel 0113 248 4044, email natleodis@googlemail.com

North Riding Vegetarians & Vegans
Cottage no 3, Arrathorne, Bedale, North Yorkshire DL8 1NA, tel 0845 458 4714, email vegan@phonecoop.coop

Sheffield & District (South Yorkshire)
email sheffveg@daize.plus.com

Scotland

Aberdeen Vegetarian Information Centre
17 Howburn Place, Aberdeen AB11
6XT, tel 01224 573034, email
george_rodger1940@yahoo.co.uk

Around Ayrshire Vegetarian Info Centre
tel 07826 29227, email
audreyk90@aol.com

Clyde Coast (South) Information Centre
Old Sawmill Cottage, Kilkerran,
Maybole KA19 7PZ, tel 01655 740451,
email kilkerran@breathemail.net

East Lothian Veggies
44 Gourlaybank, Haddington, East
Lothian EH41 3LP, tel 01620 823643,
email elveggies@lindasneddon.co.uk

Edinburgh Vegetarians and Vegans
36 Ardmillan Terrace, Edinburgh
EH11 2JL, tel 0131 337 2513, email
mail@davidharrington.org.uk

Glasgow & District Vegetarian
Information Centre
66 Bellahouston Drive, Glasgow G52
1HQ, tel 0141 882 5650 (evenings),
email gedandmary@hotmail.com

Highland Veggies & Vegans
tel 01997 421109, email
info@highlandveggies.org

Morayshire Vegetarian & Vegan Info
Centre
Hamewith, Mount Street, Dufftown,
Keith, Banffshire AB55 4FH, tel 01340
820292, email UGHamewith@aol.com

Tay Veggies
58 Riverside Road, Wormit, Newport
on Tay, Fife DD6 8LJ, email
tayveggies@gmail.com

Wales

Bridgend Vegetarian Information Centre
2 Fairways, North Cornelly, Bridgend,
Glamorgan CF33 4DH, tel 01656
742008, email
bryn.mor@hotmail.co.uk

Caldicot Vegetarian Info Centre
1 Vicarage Gardens, Caerwent, nr
Caldicot, Gwent NP26 5BH, tel 01291
424984

Cardiff and the Vale Vegetarian Group
19 Pomeroy Street, Cardiff CF10 5GS,
tel 07790 742868, email cardiff-vale-
vegetarians@hotmail.co.uk

Chester & Clwyd Vegetarian Group
Nant Yr Hafod Cottage, Hafod
Bilston, Llandegla, Clwyd LL11 3BG,
tel 01978 790442, email
indesigneko@aol.com

Powys Vegetarian Info Centre
20 Ffordd Mynydd Griffiths,
Machynlleth, Powys SY20 8DD, tel
01654 702562

South West Wales Vegetarian Group
Glanrhydw Cottage, Cloigyn,
Pontantwn, Kidwelly, Carmarthenshire
SA17 5NB, tel 01267 232733, email
grahamesme.goddard@btinternet.com

West Wales Vegetarians
Bron y Garn, Wallis, Haverfordwest,
Pembrokeshire SA62 5RA, tel 01437
731604, email
monica.adrian@btinternet.com

VisitBritain offices

Overseas readers: your nearest VisitBritain (previously the British Tourist Authority) office will be pleased to provide you with maps, guides and travel advice. General information as well as the offices' e-mail and website addresses can be found at www.visitbritain.com while the Britain and London Visitor Centre, 1 Regent Street, London SW1Y 4XT can help with travel information once you have arrived in this country.

VisitBritain offices

Overseas readers: your nearest VisitBritain office will be pleased to provide you with maps, guides and travel advice. General information as well as the offices' email and website addresses can be found at www.visitbritain.com while the Britain and London Visitor Centre, 1 Regent Street, London SW1Y 4XT can help with travel information once you have arrived in this country. Please address post to VisitBritain at the relevant address.

AUSTRALIA
Level 3, Suite 2, 32 Walker Street, North Sydney, NSW 2060

BELGIUM
Square Vergote 14, Brussels 1200

BRAZIL
Rua Ferreira de Araujo 741, 1 Andar, Pinheiros, Sao Paulo, SP 05428-002

CANADA
160 Bloor Street East, Suite 905, Toronto, Ontario M4W 1B9

CHINA
c/o Cultural and Education Section, British Embassy, 4/F Landmark Building Tower, 18 North Dongsanhuan Road, Chaoyang District, 100004 Beijing
c/o Cultural and Education Section,

British Consulate General Shanghai, 1/F Cross Tower, 318 Fu Zhou Lu, 200001 Shanghai

CZECH REPUBLIC
Insignia, Konvitska 24, Prague 110 00

DENMARK
c/o British Embassy, Kastelsvej 36-40, Copenhagen 2100

FRANCE
5 étage, 7-13 Rue de Bucarest, Paris 75008

GERMANY, AUSTRIA AND SWITZERLAND
Dorotheenstrasse 54, 10117 Berlin

GREECE
29 Michalakopoulou Street, Athens 11528

HONG KONG
7/F The British Council, 3 Supreme Court Road, Admiralty

HUNGARY
1st Floor, Offices 103-105, Kalman u. 1, 1054 Budapest

INDIA
202-203 JMD Regent Square, 2nd Floor, Mehrauli Gurgaon Road, Gurgaon, Haryana – 122 001
c/o British Council Division, British Deputy High Commission, Mittal Tower 'C' Wing, 2nd Floor, Nariman Point, Mumbai - 400 021

c/o British Trade Office, Prestige Takt, 23 Kasturba Road Cross, Bangalore – 560 001

ITALY

Via Cesare Cantù, 20123 Milano

JAPAN

Akasaka Twin Tower 1F, 2-17-22 Akasaka, Minato-ku, Tokyo 107-0052

NETHERLANDS

Prins Hendrikkade, 1011 TD Amsterdam

NEW ZEALAND

c/o British Consulate-General Office, Level 17, IAG House, 151 Queen Street, Auckland

NORWAY

Thomas Heftyesgate 8, 0244 Oslo

POLAND

Atrium International Business Centre, Al. Jana Pawla II 23, Warsaw 00-854

PORTUGAL

Largo Rafael Bordalo Pinheiro 16, 2o piso, sala 210, 1200-396 Lisboa

RUSSIA

c/o The British Embassy, 10 Smolenskaya naberezhnaya, 121099 Moscow

SINGAPORE AND SOUTH EAST ASIA

600 North Bridge Road, #09-10 Parkview Square, 188778

SOUTH AFRICA

Regus Bryanston, The Campus, Twickenham Building, Bryanston, 2021 Johannesburg

SOUTH KOREA

c/o British Embassy, Taepyung-ro 40, Jung-gu, Seoul 100-120

SPAIN

C/ Columela 9 1 dcha, 28001 Madrid

SWEDEN AND FINLAND

Klara Norra Kyrkogata 29, 111 22 Stockholm

UNITED ARAB EMIRATES

2nd Floor, Sharaf Building, Khalid Bin Waleed Road, Dubai

USA

551 Fifth Avenue, Suite 701, New York NY 10176-0799

1766 Wilshire Blvd, Suite 1200, Los Angeles CA 90025